GW00362222

GOOD HOUSEKEEPING

Cookery Hints

GOOD HOUSEKEEPING

Cookery Hints

An A-Z of the essential facts on all aspects of

- Freezing
- Microwave cooking
- Pastry making
- Roasting
- Sauce making
- Saving time
- Rescue remedies
- Storing food

PLUS Answers to the most common "What went wrong?" queries

Susanna Tee

Published by Ebury Press
Division of The National Magazine Company Ltd
Colquhoun House
27–37 Broadwick St
London W1V 1FR

First impression 1988

Edited by Veronica Sperling
Designed by Bill Mason
Illustrations by Annie Ellis

Filmset by Advanced Filmsetters (Glasgow) Ltd
Printed and bound in Great Britain by
Mackays of Chatham PLC, Chatham, Kent

CONTENTS

HANDY REFERENCE CHARTS

INTRODUCTION

I love to cook, and as a cookery writer I find conversation with family, friends and acquaintances inevitably gets around to cookery. We discuss recipes and pass on cookery hints, and at the cookery demonstrations and radio interviews that I do, I try to answer all the numerous questions I'm asked. It was as a result of these questions that the idea of this book was conceived. Why not collect together the questions and pass on the answers in one book?

At Good Housekeeping our files are bursting with all the questions that readers of *Good Housekeeping* magazine and cookery books have asked over the years, and bursting too with the answers—from the reader who asked if it was safe to use cling film in a microwave cooker to another who asked which end she should stuff a marrow! So here they are, collected together. My special thanks go to my colleagues, Favell Bevan and Emmalee Gow, for helping me collate all the material.

This is a book to keep in the kitchen to browse through when you are waiting for the kettle to boil, or to refer to quickly when you can't remember how long it takes to cook a joint of lamb, or the correct proportions of ingredients needed to make a white sauce, or what to do if the electricity goes off and you have a freezer full of food. You will find all the answers, too, to your questions concerning microwave cookery.

The entries are listed in alphabetical order, with sub-sections within each entry to help you pinpoint your query quickly. So if you need to know what to do about the cream you have overwhipped, simply look in the section headed 'Cream'. Alternatively, if you want to know how to reduce the acidity of rhubarb, look under 'Fruit' and then 'Rhubarb' to find the answer. The extensive cross-referenced index will also help you to solve your problems quickly and easily.

Good Housekeeping Cookery Hints is packed with information and advice. I hope that I have answered your particular question and that you enjoy using the book.

SUSANNA TEE

A

ACIDULATED WATER

Q *What does it mean when a recipe refers to acidulated water?*

A Acidulated water is water to which a little lemon juice or vinegar has been added. It is used when preparing some fruits and vegetables, such as apples, celeriac and Jerusalem artichokes, to prevent them turning brown when their cut surfaces come into contact with the air.

AMERICAN INGREDIENTS, see Ingredients

AMERICAN WEIGHTS AND MEASURES, see Weights and Measures

ANGELICA

Q *Can I restore angelica that has hardened?*

A Angelica which has become hard can be softened by soaking in hot water for a few minutes.

B

BAIN-MARIE

Q *What is a bain-marie?*

A A bain-marie is used mainly for cooking delicate dishes, such as baked custards, or sauces which contain a lot of egg yolks. The purpose of a bain-marie is to keep food at a constant low temperature during cooking to prevent it cooking too quickly and curdling, and to prevent sauces from burning.

Q *How do I make a bain-marie?*

A Place the food to be cooked in a heatproof bowl or dish which will fit comfortably inside a saucepan. Fill the saucepan with sufficient hot water to come about halfway up the bowl. Aim to keep the water just below boiling point. If it does boil, cool it quickly by adding a dash of cold water.

For oven cooking, use a roasting tin to hold the cooking container, then pour in hot water to come two thirds of the way up the tin.

BAKING BLIND

Q *What does baking blind mean?*

A This is the method used for partially pre-baking the pastry case of a tart or flan before it is filled. Line the dish or tin with pastry, then prick the base with a fork. Line with kitchen foil and weigh down with baking beans. Bake blind in the oven at 200°C (400°F) mark 6 for about 15 minutes. Lift out the foil and beans and bake for a further 5 minutes until the base is just firm and lightly coloured.

BATTER

Q *How do I avoid lumpy batter?*

A Keep the batter thick by adding only a little liquid in the early stages of beating. Add the remainder later and beat until frothy and little bubbles appear. Batter made in a blender or food processor never goes lumpy.

BISCUITS (COOKIES)

Q *Can you give me some hints for making biscuits successfully?*

A
- Damp hands help when shaping ball-type biscuits.
- Space biscuits well apart on the baking sheet to allow them to spread during baking.
- For an even bake, make all biscuits the same thickness and size.
- Biscuits incorporating syrup or honey are usually soft after cooking. Leave for a few minutes to crisp before lifting on to a wire rack.
- Store biscuits in an airtight tin to keep them fresh. Do not store them with cakes as they soon lose their crispness and can take up strong flavours from other baked goods. Add one or two sugar cubes to the tin to help keep biscuits crisp. Cream fillings also soften biscuits and should only be put in just before serving.

Ingredients

Q *What flour should I use when making biscuits?*

A Plain flour is generally used for biscuits. For a 'shorter' result, a little cornflour or rice flour can replace some of the plain flour used.

Q *Which sugar should I use for making biscuits?*

A
- Caster sugar generally gives much better results than granulated as the coarse crystals of granulated give a speckled result.
- Soft dark brown sugar is preferable to demerara sugar for the same reason. Brown sugars give a richer colour and flavour than white. Golden syrup and treacle are often used in place of all or some of the sugar.

Q *Which fat (shortening) should I use for making biscuits?*

A Fat gives biscuits their 'shortness'. Butter or block margarine are suitable for all biscuits and give a rich flavour and colour. Soft tub margarine is not recommended for biscuit making. For best results, always use fat at room temperature.

Biscuit-crumb bases

Q *What can I do with broken biscuits?*

A Crush them and use to make a biscuit-crumb flan case (see below).

Q *What are the basic ingredients quantities for a biscuit-crumb base?*

A 225 g (8 oz) digestive or sweetmeal biscuits, crushed; 100 g (4 oz) butter, melted; 25–50 g (1–2 oz) sugar. (Makes a 20–23 cm/8–9 inch base.)

Q *What is the best way to crush biscuits for a flan case?*

A Put biscuits in a strong plastic bag and bash and roll well with a rolling pin. Alternatively, use a blender or food processor if you have one.

BLANCHING

Q *What is blanching?*

A Blanching is immersing food in rapidly boiling water for a short time. It is used either to destroy enzymes before freezing or preserving; to remove bitterness; to loosen skin; to make it easier to deal with the food at some later stage.

Q *Why are vegetables blanched before freezing?*

A Blanching destroys enzymes in the vegetables which cause deterioration of colour, flavour and texture—the larger the pieces of vegetable, the longer it takes for the heat to penetrate, so always follow recommended blanching times. Blanching also forces air out of the vegetables and this gives green vegetables a brighter colour and reduces the scum produced when they're eventually cooked.

Q *How is blanching done?*

A Place the prepared vegetables or fruit in a wire basket and suspend for 1–2 minutes in vigorously boiling water. Lift out the basket and plunge it straight into ice-cold water. This halts the cooking process and keeps the vegetables or fruit firm.

Q *Can you give me some tips for successful blanching?*

A
- Use a large, lidded saucepan.
- Prepare the vegetables and divide into 450 g (1 lb) batches of uniformly-sized vegetables.
- For quick cooling, have a large bowl of ice-cold water to hand. Change the water after each batch.
- The water in the blanching pan can be used for several consecutive batches but must be topped up frequently with boiling water.
- Add 25 g (1 oz) salt to the boiling water to help retain the colour of the vegetables.
- Make sure all the vegetables are totally immersed in the water; prod floating vegetables under the surface.

BOUQUET GARNI

Q *How do you make a bouquet garni?*

A Place a bay leaf, a sprig of parsley and a sprig of thyme on a small square of muslin (cheesecloth). Tie the muslin into a bag with cotton, leaving long ends of cotton to tie round the saucepan handle, or to hang over the edge of the casserole, for easy removal. Home-made bouquet garnis make unusual presents for friends.

BRANDY SNAPS

Q *I can't make brandy snaps. Can you give me some hints for success?*

A Only bake a few at a time. If the biscuits cool too much whilst still on the baking sheet and become too brittle to roll, return the sheet to the oven for a moment to soften them.

B

BREAD

BREAD

Ingredients

Q *Why doesn't my yeast work?*

A Yeast will not work if it is old or if the water used with it is too hot. Ordinary dried (active dry) yeast requires sugar to activate it, so don't forget to add a pinch to the liquid before adding the yeast.

Q *How can the close texture of home-made bread be improved?*

A Too close a texture may be due to stale yeast, or insufficient yeast for the quantity of dough, or too much salt or sugar in the mix—all these reduce the amount of carbon dioxide bubbles produced by the yeast. Always use a strong bread flour rather than general purpose softer flour. Use the right amount of water: too little inhibits dough formation, too much makes it collapse during baking.

Method

Q *My bread-making isn't always successful. Can you give me some clues as to what I might be doing wrong?*

A Here are some common problems and their possible causes:

- *A 'flying top', i.e. when the top crust breaks away from the loaf:* Under-proving; dough surface allowed to dry out during proving; oven too hot.
- *Crust split at one side of the loaf:* Loaf baked too near one side of the oven.
- *Loaf has a flat top:* Flour too soft; too little salt; dough too wet; poor shaping of dough.
- *Crust surface cracks after removal from the oven:* Over-proving; oven too hot; cooling in a draught after baking.
- *Dough collapses when put into the oven:* Over-proving.
- *Heavy, close texture; poor volume:* Flour too soft; too much salt; insufficient kneading or proving; yeast killed by rising in too hot a place.
- *Coarse, open texture:* Too much liquid; over-proving; oven too cool.
- *Uneven texture with large holes:* dough not knocked back (punched down) properly; dough left uncovered during rising.
- *Sour, yeasty flavour and smell of alcohol:* Over-proving; too much yeast; stale yeast, or fresh yeast creamed with sugar.
- *Bread stales quickly and is crumbly:* Too much yeast; flour too soft; rising too quickly in too hot a place; under-rising; over-proving.

Q *Do I really have to knead dough for as long as it says in the recipe?*

A Kneading dough strengthens the gluten (protein) in the flour. Gluten has a stretchy, rubbery quality and forms tiny bubbles which are filled with carbon dioxide released by the yeast. When heated, the gluten expands and traps the carbon dioxide in the dough. The gluten then sets and forms the 'frame' of the bread. A well-kneaded dough will result in a well-risen, even-textured loaf.

Q *Can you tell me how to achieve different finishes to my home-made bread?*

A

- If a crusty finish is desired, bread or rolls can be brushed before baking with a glaze made by dissolving 10 ml (2 level tsp) salt in 30 ml (2 tbsp) water.

- For a shiny finish, the surface should be brushed with beaten egg or beaten egg and milk. Sprinkle with poppy seeds or sesame seeds if liked.
- For a soft finish, dust the bread or rolls with flour before baking.
- Some breads and yeast buns are glazed after baking to give them a sticky finish. To do this, brush the bread with warmed honey or a syrup made by dissolving 30 ml (2 level tbsp) sugar in 30 ml (2 tbsp) water and bringing to the boil.

Q *Is there anything I can do with my bread dough to stop it rising if I haven't got time to bake it?*

A Yes, you can store yeasted doughs in the refrigerator for up to 48 hours after the first kneading. This will slow down the rising. When ready to bake, just knock back (punch down) the dough, shape into loaves, place in greased tins and leave to rise in a warm place until doubled in size. Bake as instructed in the recipe.

This also means that you don't have to get up at five in the morning to make fresh bread for breakfast. Leave the bread for its final rising in the refrigerator and bake in the morning after allowing it to come back to room temperature.

Storage

Q *Can I freeze unbaked bread dough?*

A Although frozen dough will not result in the perfect loaf, it is possible to freeze some for an emergency. The best time to freeze dough is when it has risen once, been knocked back (punched down) and shaped and is in the tin ready to rise for the second time. Just place each tin in a good-sized, oiled plastic bag, squeeze out the air, tie the bag leaving 2.5 cm (1 inch) space above the dough, and put it into the freezer. To thaw, place the frozen loaf, still in its bag, in a warm—not too hot—place and leave to thaw and rise to double its size. It will then be ready for baking.

Q *What is the best way to store fresh bread without a freezer?*

A Brown bread can be kept for four or five days if wrapped loosely in a plastic bag and stored at room temperature—don't seal the bag as this will encourage mould growth. Treat white bread in the same way, but wrap it more tightly and store it in a cool place or the refrigerator.

Stale Bread

Q *Is there any way to freshen up slightly stale bread?*

A Sprinkle it with water, wrap in kitchen foil and place in the oven at 220°C (425°F) mark 7 for 5–10 minutes.

Q *Can you give me some ideas for using up stale bread?*

A
- Make a bread and butter pudding.
- Make into breadcrumbs and store in the freezer for future use. (Ideal for stuffings.)
- Place crusts in the oven to dry when the oven is still warm from other cooking. When grated, the crumbs can be used to make toppings and coatings for many dishes.

BREADCRUMBS

Q *Is there a quick method of making toasted breadcrumbs?*

A Yes. Toast thin slices of bread, put in a plastic bag, and roll with a rolling pin to form breadcrumbs. Alternatively, if you have one, use a blender or food processor.

C

CAKES

Cake tins

Q *Why do most cake recipes tell you to prepare the cake tin first? It's a job I don't like doing so I leave it to the end!*

A If you spend time preparing cake tins *after* the mixture is ready the raising agent will start to work before the cakes reach the oven resulting in a poor rise. A handy hint is to cut out several layers of paper, for lining cake tins, at one time to save the chore next time you are baking.

Q *Is it better to use butter or oil to grease a cake tin?*

A If you use vegetable oil, the cake is less likely to stick.

Q *How do I adapt a cake recipe to make it in an unconventionally shaped tin?*

A To make an unconventionally shaped fruit or sponge cake, such as a numeral or a heart shape, the amount of cake mixture needed can be worked out from the capacity of the tin. Fill the tin with water and, for every 600 ml (1 pint) the tin will hold, use fruit or Victoria sandwich mixture made with the ingredients listed below. Multiply the quantities as required. When filling the tin with water, remember only to fill it as deep as you want the finished cake to be—not necessarily to the top.

Fruit cake
150 g (5 oz) currants
50 g (2 oz) sultanas
50 g (2 oz) seedless raisins
12 glacé cherries, halved
45 ml (3 level tbsp) chopped mixed peel
100 g (4 oz) plain flour
1.25 ml ($\frac{1}{4}$ level tsp) ground mixed spice
75 g (3 oz) butter or margarine
75 g (3 oz) soft brown sugar
1$\frac{1}{2}$ eggs, beaten
Bake at 150°C (300°F) mark 2.

Victoria (basic butter) sandwich
50 g (2 oz) butter or margarine
50 g (2 oz) caster sugar
1 egg, beaten
50 g (2 oz) self raising flour
Bake at 180°C (350°F) mark 4.

It is difficult to give an accurate guide to cooking times for cakes baked in odd-shaped containers because the more contact the heat has with the tin sides, the faster it cooks.

Ingredients

Q *What are the basic ingredients quantities for a Victoria sandwich?*

A 100 g (4 oz) self raising flour, 100 g (4 oz) butter or block

margarine, 100 g (4 oz) caster sugar and 2 large (size 2) eggs. (Makes two 18 cm/7 inch sandwich cakes.)

Q *What are the basic ingredients quantities for a rubbed-in cake?*

A 225 g (8 oz) self raising flour, 2.5 ml ($\frac{1}{2}$ level tsp) salt, 75–100 g (3–4 oz) butter or block margarine, 75 g (3 oz) sugar, 1 egg and about 150 ml ($\frac{1}{4}$ pint) milk. (Makes one 18 cm/7 inch round cake.)

Q *What is the best sugar to use for cakes?*

A Caster sugar gives the creamed mixture greater volume and yields a lighter sponge because it dissolves readily.

Q *How do you stop glacé cherries sinking in a fruit cake?*

A Rinse them in warm water, then dry thoroughly and dust with some flour (from that weighed out for the cake) before adding to the mixture.

Baking

Q *How can you tell when a cake is cooked?*

A Press the top lightly with the tip of your finger. If the mixture springs back, the cake is cooked. Another method is to pierce the cake with a fine warmed skewer. If it comes out clean, with no mixture clinging to it, the cake is ready. Also, the sides of a cake tend to shrink away slightly from the tin when it is cooked.

Q *What can I use instead of a skewer to test when a cake is cooked?*

A A strand of uncooked spaghetti works equally well.

Q *How do you prevent large rich fruit cakes from over-browning?*

A Place the tin on layers of brown paper or newspaper on a baking sheet and, about halfway through cooking or when necessary, cover the cake with a piece of thick brown paper.

Method

Q *What is the best way to mix large quantities of mixture, such as for a Christmas cake?*

A Use your hands!

Q *How do you turn out large sponge or heavy fruit cakes successfully?*

A
- Loosen a large sponge cake from the baking tin by placing the tin on a damp cloth when it is removed from the oven. Leave for 5 minutes and it will turn out easily.
- Leave heavy fruit cakes to cool in the tin before turning out. It is essential to line the tin with a double thickness of greaseproof paper and to grease well.

Q *Is there an easy way to split a cake evenly into layers?*

A Measure halfway up the side of the cake and insert cocktail sticks about 2.5–4 cm (1–1½ inches) apart all around the cake. Rest a long serrated knife on the cocktail sticks and use them as a guide while slicing across.

What went wrong?

Q *Not every cake I make is a success. Can you tell me what I might be doing wrong?*

A There are many reasons for disappointment. Here are some of them, with suggested causes:

- *Badly cracked or peaked top:* Too much raising (leavening) agent; too much mixture (batter) in tin; mixture too wet or too dry; oven too hot; cake too near top of oven.
- *Top sunk in middle:* Too much raising agent; over-creaming of fat and sugar; over-beating after egg added; mixture too wet; tin too small; under-baking; oven too cool; slamming oven door during baking!
- *Over-browning of top; hard crust:* Oven too hot; over-baking; cake too near top of oven; tin too large; too much sugar; fruit cake needing several hours' baking not protected with paper.
- *Insufficient browning:* Mixture too wet; under-baking; oven over-loaded; insufficient sugar or egg.
- *Cakes sticking to tin, or sides and bottom too brown:* Poor

quality tin; tin insufficiently greased and/or lined.

- *Crusty ring round sides of cake:* Tin over-greased.
- *Speckling on top of cake:* Raising agent and flour poorly blended; too much sugar; granulated sugar used; insufficient creaming.
- *Tunnelling in centre of cake and uneven texture:* Over-mixing or uneven mixing when adding flour or liquid; mixture too dry, causing air pockets; raising agent and flour poorly blended.
- *Fruit sunk:* Mixture too wet; fruit wet; glacé fruit syrupy; fruit too large and heavy for mixture; oven too cool; opening oven too soon; too much raising agent.
- *Coarse texture:* Fat not rubbed in or creamed properly; inadequate mixing; too much raising agent; oven too cool.
- *Rubbery texture:* Over-mixing; too much egg and/or milk.
- *Dry, crumbly texture, and cake stales rapidly:* Mixture too dry; fat not rubbed in or creamed sufficiently; too much raising agent; baking too slow.
- *Close texture:* Too little raising agent; too much fat, egg or flour; mixture too dry or too wet; over-mixing; inadequate creaming and/or beating; oven too hot; under-baking.
- *Uneven rise:* Oven incorrectly preheated; oven shelf, or oven itself, not level; cake not in centre of oven and/or oven shelf.
- *Small cakes spreading:* Mixture too wet; not enough fat; too much or too little raising agent; too much mixture in cases; oven too cool.

Q *Why don't my whisked sponge cakes rise?*

A It is vital to whisk the egg and sugar over a bowl of hot, not boiling, water. (This is not necessary when using an electric mixer, but take care not to beat more air out than in, by setting the speed too fast.) You should continue whisking until the mixture is light, white and very fluffy. The mixture is ready when it is thick enough to leave a trail on the surface when the whisk is lifted out.

Decorating

Q *Can you tell me a quick way to decorate a cake?*

A • The quickest way is to put a paper doily on top of the cake, sprinkle with icing sugar, then carefully remove the doily. The larger the holes in the pattern of the doily, the more effective the decoration will be.

- For a professional finish to a simple cake, dredge the top heavily with icing sugar and mark lines on it by 'branding' with a very hot metal skewer. (Protect your hand with a thick oven glove.) The lines can be parallel or criss-cross.
- To decorate an iced cake, press a wire cooling rack lightly on to the icing, then remove carefully. Place a silver ball dragee or a glacé cherry in each section. This makes the cake look attractive but it's simple to do.

Q *I want to marzipan a fruit cake but the top is too rounded. What should I do?*

A Cut it off level and turn the cake upside-down to prevent crumbs getting in the marzipan.

Storage

Q *How do you put a butter cream-covered cake in a tin for storing?*

A Place the cake on the up-turned lid, then cover with the tin or container, so that the cake tin is upside down—but don't forget to tell the family!

Q *What is the best way to store leftover wedding cake?*

A The top tier—plus any surplus from another tier—should be wrapped tightly in greaseproof paper and then in kitchen foil. If it is kept for longer than 2 months, it should be stripped of marzipan and icing and then re-iced shortly before it is required. Anoint the cake with a little brandy beforehand.

Successful failures!

Q *Do you have any suggestions for making use of a cake that didn't cook successfully?*

A
- Use it in a trifle.
- Make into crumbs and use for rum truffles.
- For a delicious pudding, roughly crumble the cake and put it in a soufflé dish. Pour over a little orange juice and add a can of blackcurrants with their juice. Sprinkle with cin-

namon and nutmeg and leave to soak overnight. Just before serving, decorate with whipped cream.

Q *Help! What do I do with my sunken cake?*

A If your cake sinks disastrously in the centre, cut out the middle and fill with fruit and whipped cream.

CANNED FOODS

Q *How long can I store various canned foods?*

A Canned foods can be stored for a long time. Even after the times suggested below, foods should still be safe to eat although there may be a slight change in colour, texture, aroma or flavour.

- Milk products, including evaporated milk, cream and milk puddings—*one year*
- Prunes—*one year*
- Rhubarb—*one year*
- New potatoes—*eighteen months*

- Blackberries, gooseberries, plums, blackcurrants, raspberries and strawberries—*eighteen months*
- Vegetables (apart from new potatoes)—*two years*
- Other fruits—*two years*
- Baked beans—*two years*
- Pasta products—*two years*
- Soups—*two years*
- Ready-made meals—*two years*
- Hot meat products—*two years*
- Solid pack cold meat products—*five years*
- Fish in oil—*five years*

CASSEROLES

Q *How do I remove the fat from the top of a casserole?*

A While the casserole is still hot, blot up the fat from the surface with a piece of absorbent kitchen paper. If the casserole is left to cool, the fat will rise to the surface, set and can then be removed before reheating.

Q *What is the best way to reheat a casserole?*

A Reheat casseroles by bringing them to the boil and simmering for 15 minutes. Keeping meat warm for long periods without boiling may encourage the growth of fresh bacteria.

Q *I've broken the lid of my casserole; what can I use instead?*

A Try using kitchen foil or a baking sheet.

CHEESE

Cooking

Q *What cheese should I use for cooking?*

A Choose a hard, mature cheese—the stronger flavour means you need less.

Q *What is the best way to cook dishes with cheese in them?*

A Always cook cheesy dishes over a gentle heat and never allow them to boil, otherwise the cheese will turn stringy.

Serving

Q *What is the best way to serve cheese?*

A Cheese, like red wine, should be brought to room temperature before eating. If used straight from the refrigerator it will lack flavour so take it out about 1 hour before serving.

Q *How should I serve a whole Stilton?*

A Don't scoop out the centre and leave the outside edge to dry out and harden. Take a full horizontal slice from the top and divide it into wedges.

Storing

Q *What is the best way to store cheese?*

A Wrap cheese carefully in kitchen foil, keeping different kinds of cheese separately. Store in the refrigerator or in a cool place in a covered, ventilated container.

Q *How do I store half a Stilton?*

A Cover it with a moist cloth dipped in brine and store it at 7–10°C (about 45–50°F)—the temperature of a cool larder, or even a brick or stone garage if you protect the cheese from fumes. It should remain in good condition for about 14 days. In the refrigerator, Stilton will keep for up to 1 month if you wrap it closely in kitchen foil to prevent it from drying out.

Buying blue cheese

Q *What should I look out for when buying blue cheese?*

A Blue cheeses should be evenly veined, with no brown discoloration beneath the rind. Blues ripen from the centre out so are at their best when the internal mould reaches the edge.

Leftover cheese

Q *What can I do with any leftover pieces of cheese?*

A Grate them and store in a container in the refrigerator for sprinkling on soups and pasta dishes.

CHOCOLATE

Q *Can you give me some hints for melting chocolate?*

A
- Break the chocolate into small pieces so that it melts evenly.
- Never melt chocolate over direct heat. The flavour will be impaired and it will go hard and grainy if it becomes too hot. Instead, break the chocolate into a small heatproof bowl, stand it over a saucepan of hot water and heat gently until the chocolate begins to melt. (Or use a double boiler.) Stir frequently.
- Chocolate can be melted with a small amount of liquid (not more than 15 ml/1 tbsp), but if the liquid is added after the chocolate has melted it will go grainy. If this should happen, you may be able to improve it by adding a little butter.

Q *How do I make chocolate curls for decorating desserts and cakes?*

A Using a potato peeler, pare thin curls from the edge of a block of chocolate. The chocolate should be at room temperature, not straight from the refrigerator.

CHRISTMAS PUDDING

Q *Can I add charms to a cooked Christmas pudding?*

A Yes. Wrap them in greaseproof paper and push them gently into slits in the pudding when it is cold. The slits will close up when the pudding is reheated.

COFFEE

Q *Which grade of ground coffee should I use?*

A Choose the right grade for your method of coffee-making: medium ground for jug, cafetière or percolator; fine ground for filter or espresso.

COLOURING

Q *What is the best way to add food colouring?*

A Use the tip of a fine skewer or a wooden cocktail stick dipped into the colouring to add just a drop at a time. Add it very gradually, as just one drop can be too much.

COOKIES, see BISCUITS

CREAM

Q *Can you give me some hints for whipping cream?*

A
- Always chill bowl and whisk before whipping. This will help to prevent the cream becoming granular in texture, particularly in warm weather.
- Whip cream quickly at first until it takes on a matt finish, and then more slowly. For greatest volume, stop whipping when the cream just holds its shape on the whisk.

Q *I don't have enough double cream for whipping; is there anything I can do to make it go further?*

A
- If the cream is to be used at once, add the white of an egg to increase its bulk.
- Whip the cream with 15 ml (1 tbsp) milk for each 150 ml ($\frac{1}{4}$ pint) double cream.

Q *What can I do with over-whipped cream?*

A
- If only slightly over-whipped, it can be improved by adding a little milk.
- If you have really over-whipped the cream, it will begin to separate into butterfat and buttermilk. This is a rather expensive way of making butter, but nonetheless it can be a very delicious way of avoiding a disastrous waste! Once whipped, cover the butter and put it into the refrigerator until ready to use.

Q *If I mix double and single cream together, will I get whipping cream?*

A Yes. Whip together equal quantities.

Q *If a recipe requires soured cream, is there anything I can substitute for it when I haven't any?*

A Yes. Add some lemon juice to fresh single cream and leave in a warm place for about 30 minutes. Add 15 ml (1 tbsp) to 300 ml (½ pint) cream.

CREPES, see PANCAKES

CRUMBLE

Q *What are the basic ingredients quantities of a crumble topping?*

A 100 g (4 oz) plain or self raising flour, 50 g (2 oz) butter or block margarine and 25–50 g (1–2 oz) sugar.

CURRY

Q *How do I cool down a too-hot curry?*

A Add natural yogurt, soured cream, milk, lemon juice or potato, or a combination of these.

CUSTARD

Q *What are the basic ingredients quantities for making an egg custard?*

A *For pouring custard:* 4 eggs, 600 ml (1 pint) milk, 25 g (1 oz) sugar
For baked custard: 3 eggs (or 2 whole eggs and 1 yolk), 600 ml (1 pint) milk, 25 g (1 oz) sugar

Q *How can I avoid curdled egg custard?*

A Add just a little cornflour to the sugar and eggs mixture before pouring on the warmed milk and cooking—quantities to use are 5 ml (1 level tsp) cornflour for each 600 ml (1 pint) custard.

Q *How do I prevent a skin forming on custard?*

A Sprinkle the surface with caster or icing sugar. Stir in before using. However, remember that the amount of sugar in the custard should be reduced by the amount used for sprinkling.

E

EGGS

Choosing

Q *I'm confused about the different sizes of eggs. When a recipe uses large eggs, what size should I buy?*

A The following chart will help you.

<table>
<tr><th colspan="2">Old (ounces)</th><th colspan="2">New (grammes)</th></tr>
<tr><td rowspan="3">Large</td><td rowspan="3">$2\frac{3}{16}$ oz and over</td><td>SIZE 1</td><td>70 g and over</td></tr>
<tr><td>SIZE 2</td><td>65–70 g</td></tr>
<tr><td>SIZE 3</td><td>60–65 g</td></tr>
<tr><td rowspan="2">Standard</td><td rowspan="2">$1\frac{7}{8}$–$2\frac{3}{16}$ oz</td><td>SIZE 4</td><td>55–60 g</td></tr>
<tr><td>SIZE 5</td><td>50–55 g</td></tr>
<tr><td>Medium</td><td>$1\frac{5}{8}$–$1\frac{7}{8}$ oz</td><td>SIZE 6</td><td>45–50 g</td></tr>
<tr><td>Small</td><td>$1\frac{1}{2}$–$1\frac{5}{8}$ oz</td><td rowspan="2">SIZE 7</td><td rowspan="2">under 45 g</td></tr>
<tr><td>Extra small</td><td>under $1\frac{1}{2}$ oz</td></tr>
</table>

Q *Are brown eggs better for you than white eggs?*

A No. Although brown eggs have the image of being more wholesome than white eggs, virtually the only difference between brown and white eggs is the price, and even that is due to consumer demand. The colour of the egg is determined by the hen that produced it.

Q *How do I tell if an egg is fresh?*

A
- Put the uncooked egg in a bowl of water. If it lies on the bottom, it is fresh; if it tilts it is older (and should be used for frying or scrambling rather than boiling); if it floats it is likely to be bad.
- If you are using a lot of eggs in a particular dish, remember

to crack eggs individually into a cup first before adding them to other ingredients. It can be very wasteful to throw everything away if one of the eggs is bad.

Q *How do I get an egg out of a carton in which it has stuck?*

A Wet the carton, then the egg will come out without breaking.

Cooking

Q *What is the best way to boil an egg?*

A Let them just simmer gently. Rapid boiling causes tough whites and rubbery yolks.

Q *How long should I boil an egg for?*

A Cooking time for medium (size 4) eggs, timed from when the water begins to simmer:

	Added to hot water	**Added to cold water**
Whites set but not hard, yolks runny	3–4 mins	4–5 mins
Whites hard, yolks just beginning to set at edges	4–5 mins	5–6 mins
Whites and yolks hard and suitable for cutting	8–10 mins	10 mins

Q *How can I avoid eggs cracking when I boil them?*

A Make a pinhole in the shell first.

Q *Can I still boil an egg that has cracked?*

A
- The white will not escape if you parcel the egg in foil before boiling.
- Alternatively, add a few drops of vinegar or lemon juice to the cooking water.

Q *When I hard-boil an egg, how do I prevent a grey ring forming between the yolk and the white?*

A Do not over-cook the eggs. As soon as they are taken from the pan, crack them to let the steam escape and plunge into cold water. Leave for several minutes.

Q *How can I get the yolks to set in the centre of hard-boiled eggs?*

A Using a wooden spoon, stir the eggs gently for the first 3 minutes of cooking time.

Q *I find hard-boiled eggs difficult to shell. Have you a hint to help me?*

A If you add a spoonful of vinegar to the boiling water, the eggs will be easier to shell.

Q *How do I prevent scrambled eggs from becoming rubbery?*

A Remove the eggs from the heat *before* they are fully set as they will continue cooking in their own heat.

Whisking

Q *Why is it that, sometimes, when I try to whisk egg whites, they stubbornly refuse to whisk?*

A This will happen if there is even the tiniest hint of grease on the bowl or whisk. Rubbing a cut lemon round the inside of the bowl ensures grease is removed.

Q *How can I achieve more volume when whisking egg whites?*

A
- Add a pinch of salt.
- Allow eggs stored in the refrigerator to warm up at room temperature before whisking. You will achieve a better volume because egg whites at room temperature absorb more air.
- Use a chilled bowl and a chilled whisk, in a cool place. The cooler the air incorporated, the more the mixture will rise.

Separating

Q *Is there a reliable method of separating an egg?*

A Instead of tipping the egg from one half-shell to another, tip it into the palm of your hand and let the egg white run through your fingers.

Q *When separating an egg, what do I do if a piece of shell gets into either the yolk or the white.*

A Remove the offending fragment with a larger piece of egg shell. This works wonderfully well as the egg shell has a sharp edge.

Leftover eggs

Q *Can I do anything with one egg white that I have left over?*

A
- A single egg white can easily be frozen in an ice cube container, then taken out and packed (label it clearly); it will store well for up to 6 months. It is best allowed to thaw in the refrigerator.
- For a delectably different effect, frost the rims of glass compote dishes by dipping them first in a saucer of lightly mixed egg white and then in caster sugar.

Q *How do I store leftover egg yolks?*

A Put them in a small bowl, cover with water and store in the refrigerator for up to 5 days.

Q *What can I do with leftover egg yolks?*

A
- Here are some ideas: mayonnaise and hollandaise sauces; add to mashed potatoes; use to enrich white sauces; add to soups; use for pastry, crème brûlée, ice cream and biscuits.
- You can also use them to replace whole eggs in dishes where the white is not needed to aerate the other ingredients. Two yolks plus 15 ml (1 tbsp) water equals one whole egg.

Storing

Q *What is the best way to store eggs?*

A Store, pointed end down, in a wire basket or rack, in a cool place or the refrigerator for up to 3 weeks. Do not store eggs too closely to cheese or other strong-smelling foods since they quickly absorb smells through the pores of their shells.

F

FISH AND SEAFOOD

Buying

Q *What should I look out for when I buy fresh fish?*

A Fresh fish should have bright, clear eyes, red gills and bright, tight scales or shiny skin. Flesh should be firm and spring back when prodded. Fresh fillets or steaks should appear freshly cut, without a dried or brownish look, and should have a firm texture. All fresh fish will have a fresh, mild odour.

Q *What should I look out for when I buy frozen fish?*

A Frozen fish should be tightly wrapped and solidly frozen with clear colour and no ice crystals, discoloration or brownish tinge. Odour, if any, should be mild. The coating on breaded (crumbed) fish should be crisp, not soggy.

Storing

Q *What is the best way to store fresh or frozen fish?*

A Wrap fresh fish loosely, keep refrigerated and use within a day. Frozen fish that is not to be used immediately should be stored in the freezer in its wrapping. Do not thaw and refreeze it.

Preparation

Q *How do I prevent a fish slipping about when I skin it?*

A Dip your thumb and forefinger in salt to give a firmer grip.

Q *How do I skin a cooked fish?*

A Slip a knife between the edge of the fish skin and the flesh and gently peel off the skin. Turn the fish over and remove the skin from the second side. Ease out all the fine bones.

Q *How do I bone a round fish?*

A Before boning a round fish, first remove the head, if you wish, then gut the fish. Open out the fish and flatten it on a wooden board, tummy side down, spreading out the sides. Run your thumb firmly down the backbone to loosen it from the flesh. Turn the fish over and carefully lift off the backbone and attached bones, starting from the head end and using the point of a knife if necessary.

Cooking and serving

Q *How much fish should I serve per person?*

A Allow about 175–225 g (6–8 oz) raw fish and 125–175 g (4–6 oz) cooked fish per person, remembering that the head and tail are wasted.

Q *How can I tell when fish is cooked?*

A Fish should be cooked quickly for just long enough to coagulate the protein and bring out its flavour. Over-cooking makes it tough and tasteless. Fish is cooked as soon as the flesh turns opaque and milky all the way through, and flakes easily when tested with a fork.

Q *What does* en papillote *mean?*

A Literally, 'in a paper case'—this is usually food, especially fish, that is cooked wrapped in buttered greaseproof paper or kitchen foil. The juices of the food are preserved in the parcel and served with the food. This method is usually used for small fish with a delicate flavour, such as red mullet or salmon.

Anchovies

Q *Is it possible to decrease the saltiness of anchovies?*

A Soaking in a little milk for about 30 minutes will help.

Mussels

Q *How do you prepare mussels?*

A Soak mussels in salted water with a sprinkling of oatmeal for about 1 hour to get rid of the grit, then drain and scrub them under cold running water. Scrape off any mud, barnacles, seaweed and 'beards' with a small, sharp knife. Discard any mussels which do not close when tapped before cooking, and any which do not open after cooking.

Q *How much less do mussels weigh once they are shelled?*

A About half as much, eg. 900 g (2 lb) mussels in their shells gives 450 g (1 lb) after shelling.

Prawns

Q *What weight of prawns is left after peeling 225 g (8 oz)?*

A Prawns lose about 60% of their weight when peeled, so 225 g (8 oz) will yield about 75 g (3 oz).

Q *What is the difference between a prawn and a shrimp?*

A Prawns come in various sizes. Very small prawns are called shrimps and large prawns are called jumbo or king prawns.

Salmon

Q *My oven isn't large enough to bake a whole salmon—what can I do?*

A Cut the fish in half across the middle, then bake as for a whole fish. Reassemble on the serving dish and garnish neatly with cucumber slices to hide the cut.

Q *What is the best way to skin and bone a cooked whole salmon and still retain its shape?*

A While the fish is still hot, lay it on a clean tea-towel on a firm surface. Snip the skin below the head and above the tail and gently peel it off. Invert a serving plate over the fish and gather up the tea-towel. Turn plate and tea-towel together so that the fish is the other way up on the plate. Remove the skin from the second side. Ease out all the fine bones and leave the head and tail intact. With a sharp pointed knife, slit the fish along the backbone, without disturbing the flesh, and ease out the backbone and attached bones through the slit.

Q *At what temperature and for how long should I bake salmon?*

A Bake at 180°C (350°F) mark 4 for the following times:
Whole fish over 2.3 kg (5 lb): 8 minutes per 450 g (1 lb)
Whole fish or middle cuts from 900 g–2.3 kg (2–5 lb): 10 minutes per 450 g (1 lb)
Whole fish under 900 g (2 lb): 10–15 minutes per 450 g (1 lb)

Smoked salmon

Q *What is the best way to store smoked salmon?*

A Frozen smoked salmon—vacuum-packed, unopened and with the seal intact—will keep in good condition in the freezer for at least 6 months. To thaw, remove the packaging and re-wrap closely in foil. Store in the refrigerator for no more than 1 week. Treat vacuum-packed, non-frozen smoked salmon in the same way.

Q *How do you skin and slice smoked salmon?*

A Place the salmon fillet skin uppermost on a board and, using a very sharp long-bladed knife, start at the tail end and carefully loosen the skin without cutting into the flesh. Loosen the skin from as much salmon as you need but do not cut it off. Turn the fillet over so the skin is underneath and cut into thin slices. Cover the remaining salmon with the flap of skin to prevent it drying out.

FLOUR

Q *If I haven't any self raising flour, can I make it by adding baking powder to plain flour?*

A Yes. Add 12.5 ml (2½ level tsp) baking powder to every 225 g (8 oz) plain flour. Alternatively, add 2.5 ml (½ level tsp) bicarbonate of soda and 5 ml (1 level tsp) cream of tartar. Sift together several times before use.

Q *Lots of recipes call for seasoned flour; how do I make it?*

A Add plenty of salt and pepper to flour, then store in a screw-topped jar or labelled flour dredger ready for action. If coating meat in seasoned flour, put everything in a plastic bag and shake together.

FREEZING

The freezer

Q *What do the various star ratings mean on a freezer?*

A Star ratings distinguish a true food freezer (with four stars) from those designed purely for storing ready-frozen foods, which are rated as follows:

*** Ready-frozen food will keep for up to 3 months
** Ready-frozen food will keep for up to 1 month
* Ready-frozen food will keep for up to 1 week

Q *What do I do if there is a power cut or my freezer breaks down?*

A
- Don't open the freezer door.
- Don't keep the cooker on if next to the freezer.
- Insulate the freezer by wrapping it with a blanket or sleeping-bag.

- Once the power has returned, check the food to see if it has thawed and don't refreeze any that has.

Q *How can I keep down the running costs of my freezer?*

A To cut running costs, use all available freezer space. Crumpled newspaper will fill up any extra gaps.

Freezing facts

Q *Can I refreeze food once it has thawed?*

A As with all perishable foods, if frozen food is thawed and then kept at room temperature, bacteria will develop and it will become a health hazard. It is therefore not advisable to refreeze food unless it has been cooked after thawing.

Q *Is it safe to eat frozen food after the recommended storage time has expired?*

A Yes. Storage times are determined by the length of time foods can be stored frozen without any detectable change in food value, taste, colour and texture.They can be stored longer than the recommended times without becoming harmful to health, but the flavour and texture will not be as good.

Q *Do I have to use the fast-freeze switch every time I freeze something?*

A It is possible to freeze food without using the fast-freeze switch, but the faster the food is frozen the better the texture when thawed.

Q *Does freezing affect the nutritional value of food?*

A Freezing itself has virtually no effect on the nutrients in food—but the preparation can reduce the nutritional value. Keep losses to a minimum by preparing the food correctly. Thawing can also reduce the vitamin content—for example, they are lost as meat thaws. If possible, cook vegetables, fruit and fish from frozen in the minimum amount of water.

Q *Do I really have to blanch vegetables before I freeze them?*

A Some vegetables can be frozen without blanching but their keeping times tend to be shorter. These are broad (lima) beans, runner beans and sweetcorn (*3–4 weeks*); green peppers (capsicums) (*3 months*); peas (*9 months*); carrots and spinach (*12 months*). (See Blanching, page 11.)

Q *What is freezer-burn?*

A The dehydration of the surface of food which is not properly protected from the cold, dry air in the freezer. Freezer-burn will develop on meat and poultry in a punctured pack. Although it looks unattractive and, after cooking, may taste dry, it is perfectly safe to eat.

Freezing sense

Q *Can you give me some hints for successful freezing?*

A
- Always start with good quality foods and freeze them at peak freshness. Poor quality food won't improve but will deteriorate with freezing.
- Keep handling to a minimum and make sure everything is scrupulously clean. Freezing doesn't kill bacteria.
- Pay special attention to packaging and sealing. Exposure to air and moisture damages frozen foods, therefore use moisture/vapour-proof wraps of a type and size suitable for the contents.
- Cool food rapidly if it's been cooked or blanched; never put anything hot—or even warm—into your freezer.
- Freeze as quickly as possible, and in small quantities.
- Freeze in the coldest part of your freezer. Don't pack items of food to be frozen too closely together—spread them out until frozen.
- Transfer newly added items to the main part of the freezer once they've been frozen.
- Use the fast-freeze facility when freezing foods and don't forget to return the switch to 'normal' once newly added foods have been frozen, i.e. after about 24 hours.
- Maintain a steady storage temperature of −18°C (0°F) in the freezer, and don't open the door more often than necessary.
- Label and date food so that you can rotate stock. Ideally,

keep a record and tick off items as you use them, then you can tell without opening the freezer which supplies are getting low.

- Be prepared for emergencies. Make sure you know what steps to take in case of a breakdown or power cut (see page 39).
- When packing foods for freezing, exclude as much air as possible, but remember to allow appropriate headspace before sealing securely.
- Label food packages before putting them in the freezer because labels won't stick to frozen parcels.
- It is essential never to freeze more than one tenth of your freezer's capacity in any 24 hours. It is possible to freeze more, of course, but because the addition of the unfrozen food pushes up the freezer temperature, the result will be slow freezing, which should be avoided.
- Use a light hand when seasoning pre-cooked dishes to be frozen. Garlic tends to give a rather musty flavour to frozen meals.
- Use shallow rather than deep dishes.
- To simplify reheating, tape details of oven temperature, reheating time, etc, to the top of the food before freezing. If a dish is to be topped with grated cheese or bread-crumbs, or if cream is to be added, you can be very efficient and attach a note about these to the pack too—especially if someone else is doing the reheating.

Q *How can I economise on freezer containers?*

A Reduce the number of freezer cartons needed by lining those you already have with plastic bags before filling them with food. Remove the bags when the contents have frozen into an easily-stored block.

Q *I make ice cubes in the freezer part of my refrigerator but because of spillage and leaky ice-cube trays, I am always having to defrost the whole fridge. How can I avoid this?*

A Next time you defrost the fridge, find a plastic tray large enough to hold the ice-cube trays, then when it gets iced up, simply take it out, rinse off and return. This will avoid the laborious job of having to defrost the whole fridge.

Food

Q *Which foods don't freeze well?*

A
- Apart from foods which contain a high proportion of water and have a delicate cell structure (examples are lettuce, cucumber, strawberries, tomatoes, celery and watercress), there are a few foods that don't give satisfactory or reasonable frozen results. Some of these non-starters, however, can be used as part of a recipe or given special treatment, for example cucumber soup and strawberry purée.
- *Bananas* turn black. This can be improved if the flesh is masked with lemon juice and used in a recipe.
- *Caviar* should not be frozen.
- *Cooked egg custard* separates but canned custard (in a trifle, for example) freezes satisfactorily.
- *Cream cheese* or cottage cheese do not freeze satisfactorily. However, hard and blue—veined cheeses freeze well, either in the piece or grated. Allow plenty of time for thawing. Curd cheese is best frozen in retail cartons sealed with tape. Camembert and other soft cheeses should be matured before freezing.
- *Cream* does not freeze successfully when single, very thick double, or clotted. Whipping and double cream can be frozen satisfactorily. For best results, *slightly* whip and add 5–10 ml (1–2 level tsp) caster or icing sugar before whipping, if acceptable.
- *Eggs* cannot be frozen in the shell. Hard-boiled (hard-cooked) eggs become tough and watery, and the whites turn grey. Egg whites and whole beaten eggs freeze well. Separated yolks become gummy unless salt or sugar is added.
- *Hollandaise sauce*, mayonnaise and other egg-based sauces tend to separate.
- *Jam* used in large amounts or as a filling has a tendency to liquefy and soak into the surrounding food.
- *Jelly* made up in a mould will collapse when frozen. However, it can successfully be poured over sponge cake or crumbs and incorporated in made-up dishes. Aspic glazes should be added after thawing or used for coating when the item is half thawed.

- *Natural yogurt* (or home-made) separates when frozen. Flavoured sweet yogurts show little or no deterioration.
- *Potatoes* of certain types go leathery in pre-cooked frozen dishes unless mashed first. Something like a Moussaka is fine as the potatoes are masked by the cheesy sauce.
- *Sandwiches* can be frozen but avoid fillings of hard-boiled eggs (which will become rubbery), salad or mayonnaise. Bear in mind that spicy flavours, such as curry or garlic become more pronounced if frozen.

Poultry

Q *Why does poultry have to be fully thawed before it is cooked?*

A Micro-organisms called *Salmonellae* are endemic in most poultry and, if the flesh is not thoroughly cooked, can cause food poisoning. This may happen with poultry that has never been frozen but is more likely to occur with insufficiently thawed chicken, turkey, duckling or goose. The still frozen part of the bird (usually the body cavity which has a high number of *salmonellae*) remains at a relatively low temperature even though the bird appears cooked. If sufficient micro-organisms survive, or if the poultry is left at room temperature for a while, allowing them time to multiply, the *salmonellae* can cause food poisoning. The golden rules are to thaw properly and to ensure that all poultry is cooked thoroughly.

Q *What is the best method and how long does it take to thaw poultry?*

A Thaw poultry weighing up to 2.7 kg (6 lb) in the refrigerator and poultry weighing more than that at room temperature. If the giblets are inside the body cavity, remove them as soon as possible. Approximate thawing times are as follows:

Frozen weight		
up to 1.8 kg (4 lb)	12 hours	in the refrigerator
1.8–2.7 kg (4–6 lb)	15 hours	
2.7–4.5 kg (6–10 lb)	18 hours	at room temperature
4.5–6.8 kg (10–15 lb)	24 hours	
6.8–9 kg (15–20 lb)	30 hours	

Standbys

Q *Can you give me some hints for useful standbys to store in the freezer?*

A Apart from convenience foods, such as frozen vegetables, frozen orange juice, chicken joints, chops, ice creams and peeled prawns, the following are some items which you may find useful to have readily available in the freezer.

- *Bread and bread rolls:* Always a good standby to store. Sliced bread can be toasted straight from the freezer. Pitta bread too will thaw under the grill. Crusty bread should not be stored in the freezer for more than 1 week as it tends to flake.
- *Breadcrumbs:* Can be added frozen to onion sauce, stuffings and puddings which are to be cooked.
- *Casseroles and stews:* Double the recipe and freeze half for later. Most can be reheated from frozen. It is important, though, to omit vegetables (such as potatoes), pasta and rice, that go mushy during freezing. Add them when you reheat the dish. Be careful when seasoning casseroles and curries for the freezer, as freezing strengthens flavours. When a dish has been cooked and cooled, remove surplus fat before freezing to avoid rancidity. There must be enough liquid in the dish to cover the meat completely, otherwise the meat may dry out. Casseroles must be cooled thoroughly and quickly before freezing. When reheating, it is important to bring the casserole to the boil and then simmer it for 15 minutes.
- *Cheese:* Grate and freeze hard cheese in usable quantities. It can be used from frozen.
- *Chocolate curls:* Add a professional touch to both puddings and cakes.
- *Coffee beans* and ground coffee: They can be used from frozen.
- *Cream:* Whipped double (heavy) cream, piped into rosettes and then frozen, can be used to decorate puddings and cakes while still frozen. They take 10 minutes to thaw at room temperature. Sticks of frozen cream can be stirred straight into soups and sauces.
- *Croûtons:* Fried bread croûtons can be reheated from

frozen. Heat in the oven at 220°C (425°F) mark 7 for 5–10 minutes. Use to garnish soups, salads and snacks.

- *Fresh herbs:* Wrap and freeze whole sprigs and use them as they are, or crumble while still frozen to save time chopping. Alternatively, chop and freeze in ice cubes to drop straight into a dish during cooking.
- *Orange and lemon juice:* Freeze in small containers or ice-cube trays and use for drinks, cakes, dressings and sauces.
- *Orange and lemon rind:* Store small quantities of grated rind and use for flavouring.
- *Orange and lemon slices:* Open freeze, then pack. Useful for decorating foods and serving with drinks.
- *Pastry:* All types will freeze well, either as an uncooked dough or rolled out and baked. You can also freeze pastry unbaked in pies, quiches, tarts and flans. Make in bulk but pack in usable quantities. It may be more convenient to roll out raw pastry into pie lids, pie and flan cases and vol-au-vents before freezing.
- *Sandwiches:* Prepare in bulk for parties or packed lunches (see page 114).
- *Sauces:* Make large quantities of sweet or savoury sauces and freeze in usable amounts.
- *Savoury butters:* Add a luxury touch to grilled meat, fish or vegetables. Freeze in rolls and cut slices as required. Use straight from the freezer.
- *Seville oranges:* Buy when cheap and plentiful and freeze whole until you are ready to make marmalade.
- *Soups:* Make in large quantities and pack in usable amounts. Most can be reheated from frozen.
- *Stock:* Make a large quantity, boil briskly to reduce, then freeze concentrated in small quantities for convenience.
- *Vol-au-vents:* Baked or uncooked, they take little time to thaw or cook.

FRENCH DRESSING

Q *What are the ideal proportions for making French dressing?*

A The usual proportions are three parts oil to one part vinegar. Use less oil if a sharper dressing is preferred.

Q *What is the best way to store French dressing?*

A French dressing is best stored in a screw-topped jar or bottle somewhere cool, but not in the refrigerator.

FRITTERS

Q *I'm not very good at making fritters. Can you give me some tips?*

A The following are common problems and their possible causes:

- *Greasy and soggy:* Fat too cool; fritters not drained well after cooking.
- *Food inside uncooked:* Fat too hot; coating too thin or uneven; pieces of food too large.
- *Batter floats off food:* Batter too thin; food not dried before dipping in batter; fat at wrong temperature.

FRUIT

Apples

Q *How do I stop apple slices turning brown?*

A Brush or dip the cut surfaces in lemon juice.

Apricots

Q *What is the best way to stone apricots?*

A Cut them in half lengthways with a sharp knife, along the slight indentation. Twist the two halves in opposite directions to separate them and lift out the stone.

Blackcurrants

Q *What is the best way to string fresh blackcurrants?*

A Use a fork to strip the berries off the stalks. If freezing blackcurrants, open freeze them on their stalks and store frozen in a rigid container. If you give the container a good shake, most of the frozen fruit will fall off the stalks.

Coconuts

Q *How do you open a fresh coconut?*

A Bore a hole through two of the eyes at one end of the coconut. Drain off the liquid and reserve it, if wished. A coconut will crack more easily if put in the oven at 150°C (300°F) mark 2 for 20 minutes. It should crack itself while cooling, but if it doesn't tap it lightly with a hammer.

Dates

Q *How do I remove the tough skins of fresh dates?*

A Cut off the stalk end, squeeze the opposite end and the date should pop out.

Q *How can I chop dates without them sticking to the knife?*

A Dip the knife in cold water.

Grapes

Q *How do I remove pips from whole grapes?*

A Use the curved end of a clean hair-grip.

Lemons

Q *I am always surprised how little juice my lemons yield—how can I get more out of them?*

A Try and have them at room temperature before squeezing. Warm lemons yield more juice.

Q *How much juice is there in a lemon?*

A A juicy lemon gives about 45 ml (3 tbsp) juice.

Q *When I slice lemons they discolour; what can I do to prevent this?*

A When cutting lemons, use a stainless steel knife as the acid in the lemon discolours steel knives and the lemon flesh, unless wiped between each slice.

Melons

Q *How do I test if a melon is ripe?*

A When a melon is ripe, the stalk end should give very slightly when pressed, and there is a distinct aroma.

Q *I find the flavour of melon is often disappointing. How should I serve them so that their flavour is not lost?*

A Refrigerate melon for no longer than it takes just to chill it to avoid losing its delicate flavour.

Oranges

Q *How much juice is there is an orange?*

A A medium orange will yield about 60 ml (4 tbsp) juice.

Q *What is the best way to cut an orange into segments?*

A Using a sharp, serrated knife, cut off one end to make a flat base. Stand the orange on the cut end and remove peel and pith together, cutting downwards. Continue until the orange is completely free of peel and pith. Holding the orange in one hand (over a bowl to catch the drips), slide the knife between the segments and the surrounding membrane. Cut out the segments, leaving the white inner membrane behind. Finally, squeeze out any juice remaining in the membrane.

Oranges and lemons

Q *How do I add just a few drops of orange or lemon juice to a mixture?*

A Pierce one end of an orange or lemon with a cocktail stick and squeeze out the amount of juice you require. Keep the hole stopped up with the stick until you need a little juice again.

Q *What can I use orange and lemon rind in? It seems such a waste to throw the peel away.*

A
- Use the grated rind of an orange or lemon to flavour a plain cake or biscuits.
- Rub sugar cubes gently all over the skin of an orange or lemon until soaked with the oils from the zest. Crush the cubes and use in cakes, to flavour hot milk drinks or to flavour sweet sauces or custards.
- Add to the pastry for mince pies at Christmas.

Peaches

Q *What is the easiest way to peel a peach?*

A Put peaches into a pan of boiling water and count to 15 before removing and peeling. Use a potato peeler on really firm ones.

Pineapple

Q *Coring pineapple slices with a knife is very fiddly; is there an easier way?*

A A small round pastry cutter, pressed firmly over the core, does the job more efficiently. This could also be done with the circular top of an apple corer, or with the base of a large piping nozzle.

Q *Why didn't my pineapple jelly set?*

A Fresh pineapple will prevent a gelatine-based jelly from setting, due to an enzyme called bromelin found in the fresh fruit. Canned pineapple, however, lacks this enzyme and will set beautifully in gelatine.

Raspberries and strawberries

Q *Should you wash fruits, such as raspberries and strawberries?*

A Avoid washing unless absolutely necessary as this will cause loss of flavour. If you must wash them, put the fruit in a colander and gently run cold water over.

Rhubarb

Q *How can I reduce the acidity of stewed rhubarb?*

A Cook it in cold tea!

Seville oranges

Q *Can I freeze a large quantity of Seville oranges when they are in season, for making marmalade at a later date?*

A Yes, Seville oranges may be scrubbed, packed in suitable quantities and frozen whole until required for making marmalade. It is advisable to add one-eighth extra weight of oranges when freezing for subsequent marmalade-making, in order to offset pectin loss.

Strawberries

Q *What is the best way to store strawberries?*

A Strawberries will keep for several days if kept in a colander in the refrigerator, as they need air to circulate around them. Only wash the strawberries just before hulling and eating, otherwise they will absorb a lot of water.

FRUIT PIES

Q *How do I thicken the juices in a fruit pie?*

A Mix 15 ml (1 tbsp) cornflour with the quantity of sugar used for sweetening the fruit pie and it will thicken the juices as the pie cooks. It makes a fruit pie particularly good for serving cold as the filling is almost set.

FRUIT PUREE

Q *My recipe states 300 ml ($\frac{1}{2}$ pint) sieved fruit purée. How much fruit should I sieve?*

A 450 g (1 lb) soft fruits, such as raspberries or strawberries, pushed through a sieve, will give you about 300 ml ($\frac{1}{2}$ pint).

FRYING

Q *When I fry in butter, it always burns. Can I stop this from happening?*

A Yes. Use half butter and half oil. Oil can be fried at a higher temperature than butter and will stop the butter burning.

Deep frying

Q *Can you give me some hints to enable me to deep-fat fry safely?*

A
- If you deep fry in a pan on a cooker, only fill the pan one-third full.
- Never fry *wet* potatoes.
- Never leave the pan unattended.
- Watch to ensure that the fat does not get too hot.

Q *Can I keep the oil I've used for deep frying and use it again?*

A Yes, oil for deep frying can be kept indefinitely if you remember to:
- Avoid overheating it.
- Strain it after use.
- Coat all meats, including sausages, with flour, egg and

crumbs or pastry to prevent the meat juices escaping into the fat.

- Keep it out of direct sunlight.

Q *At what temperature and for how long should I deep fry food?*

A The following chart lists some common foods that are deep fried, with their temperature and time for frying:

DEEP FRYING GUIDE

Food	Temperature	Time
Chipped potatoes (French fries) 0.5 cm (¼ inch) thick	190°C (375°F)	9–10 minutes
Potato croquettes 8 cm (3½ inches) long (egg and bread-crumb coating)	190°C (375°F)	3–4 minutes
Scotch egg 8 × 8 cm (3½ × 3½ inches) (egg and bread-crumb coating)	160°C (325°F)	10 minutes
Chicken Kiev 10 × 6 cm (4 × 2½ inches) (egg and bread-crumb coating)	160°C (325°F)	15 minutes
Fish fillets 1 cm (½ inch) thick (batter or egg and breadcrumb coating)	177–188°C (350–370°F)	5–10 minutes
Doughnuts	175–180°C (350–360°F)	5–10 minutes
Whitebait, floured	177–188°C (350–370°F)	2–3 minutes

If you are frying a large quantity of food in batches, you will have to wait after frying each batch for the fat to reheat. Never allow it to over-heat.

Q *I don't have a thermometer for deep-fat frying; is it possible to test when the correct temperature of the oil has been reached?*

A Drop a small cube of bread into the oil. When it browns in 1 minute, the oil is ready to use. If there is a haze over the oil, it is too hot.

Q *If by some awful chance my deep-fat-fryer ignites, what should I do?*

A *Never never* carry the pan to the sink or garden. Immediately cover your hands with a thick cloth and place either the saucepan lid, a metal baking sheet or, best of all, a kitchen fire blanket over the fire. Turn off the heat. Leave until cool enough to handle.

G

GAME

Pheasant

Q *What is the best way to cook a pheasant?*

A A good pheasant is at its best roasted but do not roast a pheasant unless you are sure it is young. Otherwise casserole, braise or stew.

GARNISHES

Q *I know that presentation of food is important but often I don't have much time. Can you give me some ideas for quick garnishes?*

A
- *Spring onion curls:* Cut off all but 7.5 cm (3 inches) of green tops with a sharp knife and shred the tops down to the white part. Chill in iced water until the tops curl.
- *Tomato flowers:* Make four skin-deep slits halfway down the side of a cherry tomato. Place the tomato in boiling water for 30 seconds, then dip in cold water. Peel sections of skin back to make petals.
- *Lime wedge curl:* Cut a lime into eight wedges and separate the peel from the fruit three-quarters of the way down each wedge. Roll the peel under, towards the centre.
- *Radish pompoms:* Trim large radishes, leaving some leaves but slicing off roots. At the root end, slice off the tip and make cuts 1 cm ($\frac{1}{2}$ inch) deep into the radish. Cut again, this time at right angles to the first cuts for a cross-hatch effect. Chill in iced water until the sections separate.
- *Citrus shreds:* Use a zester to remove the outer peel of oranges and lemons in seconds. The long fine shreds look attractive scattered on sweet and savoury dishes.
- *Savoury butter:* Store a roll of savoury butter in the freezer. Cut off slices when required.
- *Chopped consommé:* Freeze concentrated beef consommé

until set firm, then chop with a wet knife into fine pieces and spoon round a platter of sliced pâtés or cold meats.

GELATINE

Q *How much gelatine do I need to set 600 ml (1 pint) of liquid.*

A One 11 g (0.4 oz) sachet is sufficient to set 600 ml (1 pint).

GIN

Q *I've never seen gin used in recipes. Can it be used in cooking?*

A Yes. A dish flambéed in gin will have an unusual aroma of juniper.

GOLDEN SYRUP, see SYRUP

GRAVY

Q *How do I make a quick gravy to serve with a roast?*

A For a really quick gravy, just add a little flour and sliced onion to the roasting pan before adding the joint. When the meat is cooked, you'll have a ready-made gravy, with a really good colour too.

GRINDING

Q *It takes so long to grind ingredients with a pestle and mortar. How can I do it more quickly?*

A Add coarse salt to speed up the process.

H

HERBS AND SPICES

Q *If I don't have any fresh herbs, what quantity of dried herbs should I use to replace them in a recipe?*

A 5 ml (1 tsp) chopped fresh herbs = 2.5 ml ($\frac{1}{2}$ tsp) dried;
15 ml (1 tbsp) chopped fresh herbs = 5 ml (1 tsp) dried;
45 ml (3 tbsp) chopped fresh herbs = 15 ml (1 tbsp) dried.

Q *Is there a quick way to chop herbs?*

A Yes, kitchen scissors are useful and quicker than a knife. Use them for snipping herbs such as parsley, chives, rosemary and thyme straight into the pan.

Q *How should I store dried herbs and spices?*

A Store dried herbs and spices in airtight jars away from light so that they don't lose their flavour or colour. Replace dried herbs quite frequently.

Mint

Q *I've seen people sprinkle mint with a little sugar; is this a good idea?*

A Yes. It makes chopping easier and helps to draw out the full aroma of the mint.

Q *What is the best way to use dried mint?*

A To get a better flavour from dried mint, add a little boiling water and steep for about 5 minutes before using. It makes all the difference.

HOLLANDAISE SAUCE

Q *How do I stop a hollandaise sauce from curdling?*

A Try one of the rescue remedies overleaf.

- Have ready a bowl containing a little iced water. If the sauce shows signs of curdling, put the pan or bowl of sauce in the cold water and stir briskly. Alternatively, add a small ice cube to the sauce itself, then stir quickly.
- If the sauce curdles, beat 5 ml (1 tsp) lemon juice and 15 ml (1 tbsp) curdled sauce in a warm mixing bowl until it thickens. Then beat in the remaining curdled sauce 15 ml (1 tbsp) at a time.
- If the above remedies do not work, beat two egg yolks with some seasoning in a bowl and beat in 30 ml (2 tbsp) of the curdled sauce. Cook as originally, stirring constantly, adding the rest of the mixture slowly. It will taste more eggy than usual.

HONEY

Q *Can I restore honey that has crystallised in the jar?*

A Yes. Stand the jar in a saucepan of hot water and heat very gently, stirring continuously, until the sugar crystals have melted. The same treatment can be given to crystallised syrup.

I

ICE CREAM

Q *What is the best way to serve home-made ice cream for entertaining?*

A
- For a buffet or party, freeze ice cream in scoops on baking sheets, ready to pile into a serving bowl.
- For a dinner, freeze in individual freezer-proof glasses for easy serving.
- Don't forget to soften ice cream in the refrigerator for at least 30 minutes before serving.

ICE CUBES

Q *How do I make a large quantity of ice cubes for a party?*

A Use your ice-cube trays to make lots of ice in advance. Store the cubes in a plastic bag in the freezer until required.

ICING

Q *What are the basic ingredients quantities of glacé (water) icing?*

A 225 g (8 oz) icing sugar and about 30 ml (2 tbsp) warm water or fruit juice. (Enough to cover two 18 cm/7 inch cakes.)

Q *What are the basic ingredients quantities of royal icing?*

A 450 g (1 lb) icing sugar; 2 egg whites; 10 ml (2 tsp) lemon juice and 5 ml (1 tsp) glycerine. (Enough to ice one 18 cm/7 inch cake.)

Q *I make royal icing in an electric mixer but it has a lot of air bubbles; how can I eliminate them?*

A Leave the icing, covered, in the refrigerator overnight.

Q *Can you tell me why the royal icing on my cake has discoloured?*

A The following are possible reasons for this:

- The marzipan was over-kneaded before being applied to the cake. This brings out the oils which may discolour the icing.
- Cake crumbs caught in the marzipan. Take extra care not to catch crumbs in the marzipan during rolling.
- Apricot jam (glaze) on the surface of the marzipan. Try to avoid any glaze escaping from the cake on to the outside of the marzipan.
- Marzipan insufficiently dried before applying the royal icing. Allow at least a week before icing the cake (longer if the atmosphere is particularly humid or damp). As a general rule, the marzipan should feel hard and dry to the touch.
- Using icing with too soft a consistency. Ensure that the icing is at the soft peak stage and well beaten before applying it to the cake.
- Insufficient layers of royal icing. Apply two relatively thick layers and one thin for best results.
- Prolonged and incorrect storage. After marzipan has been applied, the cake should not be iced more than a fortnight before it is needed. Once iced, store lightly covered with

plenty of greaseproof paper. Do not store the cake in a plastic airtight container which may result in moisture forming on the icing.

- Greasy equipment! Grease is royal icing's worst enemy. Ensure all icing equipment is free from grease before commencing work.

Q *How do I prevent royal icing becoming too hard?*

A You should always add 5 ml (1 tsp) glycerine for each 450 g (1 lb) icing sugar used.

Q *How do I make the butter cream icing on top of a cake smooth?*

A Use a small palette knife dipped in *hot* water to spread butter cream icing for a perfectly smooth finish.

INGREDIENTS, AMERICAN

Q *I have several American cookery books that refer to ingredients that I am unfamiliar with. Can you tell me what I should use?*

A The following glossary will help. It lists the most common ingredients that you will come across.

American	English
all-purpose flour	plain flour
angel hair pasta	vermicelli
anise	aniseed
balm	lemon balm
basilicum	basil
beet	beetroot
Belgian endive	chicory
bell peppers	red or green peppers (capsicums)
biscuit/soda biscuit/hot biscuit baking powder biscuit	scone
bluefish	mackerel
boiled dressing	salad cream
Boston sole	Dover sole
bread flour	strong flour
brownulated sugar	soft light brown sugar
cake flour	*use* plain flour
canned frosting	chocolate spread
celery knob/celery root	celeriac

champignons	button mushrooms
cilantro	coriander
coffee cream	single cream
confectioners' sugar	icing sugar
cornstarch	cornflour
double acting baking powder	baking powder
drawn butter	melted butter
dry coconut	desiccated coconut
eggplant	aubergine
enriched flour	*use* plain flour
extract	essence
farina	fine semolina
flaky pastry/flaky paste	puff pastry
flapjack	large pancake
flounder	plaice
fresh ham	leg of pork
garbanzo	chick-pea
graham flour	wholemeal flour
granulated sugar	caster sugar
ground red pepper	cayenne pepper
half-and-half	half milk, half single cream/top of the milk
hard flour	strong bread flour
heavy cream	double cream
jalapeno (sauce)	chilli (sauce)
jelly roll	Swiss roll
laos powder	*use* grated fresh root ginger
ladyfingers	sponge fingers/boudoir biscuits
light cream	single cream
lingonberries	*use* cranberries
lumpfish fillet	white fish fillet
Monteray Jack cheese	*use* mild Cheddar
oyster plant	salsify
parsley greens	parsley
paste	pastry
pastry flour	*use* plain flour
poblanos	chilli
popsicle	iced lolly
pork links	chippolatas
pie crust	shortcrust
pie dough	shortcrust
powdered sugar	caster sugar
purslane	*use* sorrel or spinach
raisin	sultana
rattrap cheese	mature Cheddar
red beet	beetroot
rock Cornish game hen	poussin/spring chicken
romaine lettuce	Cos lettuce

rutabaga	swede
scallion/green onion	spring onion
semolina	ground rice
shaohsing wine	rice wine
sherbet	sorbet/water ice
shrimps	prawns
shucked	shelled (of shellfish, peas, etc)
snow pea	mangetout
sour cherries	morello cherries
squab	young pigeon
superfine sugar	caster sugar
sweet butter	unsalted butter
tapioca/minute tapioca	cornflour
tenderloin	fillet steak
tenderloin of lamb	large loin chop
thistle oil	*use* sunflower oil
tomatillos	*use* tomatoes
two crust pie	shallow, covered pie
vanilla bean	vanilla pod
vanilla extract	vanilla essence
whipped butter	softened butter
white raisins	sultanas
xères vinegar	white wine vinegar
yellow mustard seeds	mustard seeds
yellow onion	Spanish onion
zucchini	courgette
zwieback crumbs	rusk crumbs

J K

JELLY

Q *What is the quickest way to set a jelly?*

A Dissolve the jelly in half the quantity of hot water required and add enough ice cubes to make up the full amount of liquid.

Q *What is the best way to unmould a jelly?*

A To unmould a gelatine dessert, jellied salad or savoury mousse, very carefully dip the mould in a little warm water for a second or two. This helps to loosen the jelly from the sides of the mould.

Q *What is the secret of unmoulding a jelly on to the centre of a serving plate?*

A Moisten the centre of the serving plate with cold water; if it unmoulds a little off-centre, you can then coax it into position without damaging the jelly.

KEBABS

Q *How should I cook kebabs so that the meat cooks evenly?*

A Leave a little space between cubes of meat or poultry on the skewers to help them cook more evenly and quickly.

M

MARGARINE AND BUTTER

Q *Can I use any kind of margarine or butter in a recipe?*

A When a recipe calls for margarine or butter, it usually refers to the standard block variety. Don't substitute any of the whipped varieties (including 'diet' margarines) that come in tubs—they have air beaten into them to make them fluffier, which alters the amount needed. Recipes, such as 'all-in-one' cake recipes, will specify when a soft tub margarine should be used.

MAYONNAISE

Q *How long does home-made mayonnaise keep?*

A 2–3 weeks in the refrigerator.

Q *Can I rescue mayonnaise if it begins to separate whilst I am making it?*

A Yes, don't worry, there are ways to save it. All these ways involve beating the curdled mixture into a fresh base. This base can be any one of the following: 5 ml (1 tsp) hot water; 5 ml (1 tsp) vinegar or lemon juice; 5 ml (1 tsp) Dijon mustard or 2.5 ml (½ level tsp) mustard powder (the mayonnaise will taste more strongly of mustard than usual); a fresh egg yolk to every 300 ml (½ pint) of mayonnaise. Gradually add the curdled mixture to the base, beating hard. When the mixture is smooth, continue adding the oil. (If you use an extra egg yolk you may find that you need to add extra oil.)

Q *What are the secrets of making mayonnaise successfully?*

A
- Bring the ingredients to room temperature before you start so that the mayonnaise is less likely to curdle.
- Add the oil *very* gradually.

MEAT

Buying

Q *When buying meat, what should I look out for?*

A
- *Beef* should have fat that is firm and creamy white. Lean meat should be red, well marbled with fat, firm, and with a fine grain.
- *Veal* has very little fat but it should be firm, clear and white, not watery. Lean meat should be greyish pink, firm and fine grained. It is not marbled with fat.
- *Lamb* should be well covered with clear, white, firm fat. Lean meat is pinkish-red and marbled with fat.
- *Pork* should be well covered with fat that is firm, white and free from moisture. Lean meat is greyish pink to rose, firm, fine grained and well marbled with fat.

Q *How much meat should I allow per serving?*

A Allow 175 g (6 oz) off the bone, and 225–350 g (8–12 oz) on the bone, per person.

Storing

Q *How long will fresh meat keep in the refrigerator?*

A Bacteria attacks the moist cut surfaces of meat. Therefore, a large joint will keep in good condition for up to 5 days but small cuts, such as steaks and chops, will keep for only 3 days. Minced meat, which has many cut surfaces, should be kept for no more than 24 hours.

Preparation

Q *Have you a hint for making it easier to slice raw meat?*

A Yes. Pop it into the freezer for 1–2 hours before slicing.

Q *How do I prevent raw minced meat sticking to my hands when shaping it into burgers?*

A When shaping raw minced meat into burgers, kebabs, or meatballs, wet your hands to prevent the mixture sticking.

Cooking

Q *When cooking meat, when is the best time to season it?*

A At the end of cooking. If you add salt before cooking, it draws out the juices and makes the meat tough and dry.

Carving

Q *Is there a hint for making the carving of meat easier?*

A Yes, let the cooked joint stand for 15 minutes before carving as fresh meat needs to 'settle' before it can be carved easily. This applies to poultry too.

Economy

Q *Is there anything I can do with an over-cooked joint or leftover roast meat?*

A Cut the meat into very small cubes and reheat in a curry sauce to serve with rice; mince and use meat in a bolognaise sauce to serve with spaghetti; mince, mix with a can of tomatoes and herbs, add a savoury crumble topping and bake at 190°C (375°F) mark 5 until golden brown.

Bacon

Q *I've forgotten to soak a salty piece of bacon overnight. How can I reduce the saltiness?*

A Put the bacon (or gammon) in a pan, cover with cold water and bring to the boil. Pour away the cooking water and replace with fresh cold water. Bring to the boil again, reduce the heat and simmer as usual.

Q *How do you prevent bacon rolls shrinking so much?*

A Stretch each rasher out on a board with the back of a knife for as long as it will go. Roll up as normal and secure with a wooden cocktail stick.

Q *What is the difference between smoked and unsmoked bacon?*

A Smoked bacon has been smoked after curing—hung over smouldering wood sawdust. Oak chippings or sawdust give the most distinctive flavouring. Unsmoked bacon is known as 'green', 'pale' or 'plain' bacon.

Q *How can I stop bacon rashers from curling up when I cook them?*

A Snip the fat at intervals with a pair of scissors.

Gammon and ham

Q *Should I or should I not soak a gammon these days?*

A It depends on how long the gammon has been soaked in brine, and the strength of the solution. The golden rule is to ask your butcher for his advice.

Q *What is the difference between gammon and ham?*

A Ham, strictly speaking, is the hind leg of a pig cut from the whole carcass, then cured and matured separately. A 'gammon' is the hind leg removed *after* curing. Nowadays, cooked gammon is often described as ham. More often than not, hams are cooked prior to purchase but, if not, cook as for bacon.

Q *How can I keep boiled ham moist?*

A If you let the ham cool in the water in which it has been cooked, it will help to keep it moist and succulent.

Q *How should I store a whole gammon or ham that I've bought for Christmas?*

A A fresh joint will keep for up to 10 days in a refrigerator before cooking, provided that you wrap it closely in foil to exclude as much air as possible. A vacuum-sealed joint will keep for up to 21 days. Once the joint is cooked, keep it covered and refrigerated—don't leave it in a warm room—and you can safely carry on slicing from it for about 7 days. Alternatively, cooked ham or gammon slices can be stored in the freezer.

Pork

Q *What is the secret of getting crisp crackling on roast pork?*

A Score the rind deeply with a very sharp knife and rub with oil and salt before cooking.

Steak

Q *What is the best way to tenderise steak?*

A Bash it with a meat pounder between sheets of greaseproof paper. The sheets of paper prevent the meat fibres sticking to the pounder.

Q *How long should steaks be cooked for?*

A This is very much a matter of taste, depending on how well cooked people like their steaks to be. The following chart should help.

Cooking Times for Steaks
(total in minutes)

Thickness	Rare	Medium Rare	Well-done
2 cm ($\frac{3}{4}$ inch)	5	9–10	12–15
2.5 cm (1 inch)	6–7	10	15
4 cm ($1\frac{1}{2}$ inches)	10	12–14	18–20

MERINGUES

Q *How much meringue mixture do I need to make eight meringue shells?*

A 1 egg white and 50 g (2 oz) sugar will make about eight shells;
2 egg whites and 100 g (4 oz) sugar will make about 16 shells;
3 egg whites and 175 g (6 oz) sugar will make about 24 shells.

Q *How long will cooked meringues keep for?*

A Meringues will keep well for 2 months if they are wrapped in kitchen foil and stored in an airtight container.

Q *How do I make perfect meringues?*

A
- When making meringues, the bowl should preferably be made from a 'cold' material. Copper, the professionals'

choice, produces a tremendous volume of egg white. When using a balloon whisk, choose a wide, shallow bowl; for a rotary whisk, choose a deep, narrow bowl.

- For perfect meringues, the egg whites must be at room temperature before you begin whisking. Also, the older the egg white the better!
- Any trace of fat will prevent an egg white beating up correctly.
- For best results when making meringues, add the sugar in two parts; the first should be a quarter to a half of the total, and is whisked in to retain the air, while the remainder is lightly and evenly folded in, using a metal spoon at the end.
- If you are disappointed with meringues you made because they were sticky and discoloured, the chances are you cooked them at too high a temperature. Meringues should be dried out rather than cooked, and a very low heat, such as 110°C (225°F) mark $\frac{1}{4}$, is recommended.

MICROWAVE COOKING

Almonds

Q *How can I blanch almonds in the microwave?*

A Cover 100 g (4 oz) nuts with 150 ml ($\frac{1}{4}$ pint) water. Cook on HIGH for about 2 minutes. Drain, and slip the skins off with your fingers.

Q *Can I brown flaked almonds in the microwave?*

A Yes. Spread 25–100 g (1–4 oz) flaked almonds evenly on a large plate and cook on HIGH for 8–10 minutes, stirring frequently.

Bacon

Q *Will bacon become crisp and brown in a microwave?*

A Yes, slightly, because bacon has a high fat content.

Q *Do you know any special techniques for cooking bacon in a microwave?*

A Yes. Snip the fat with scissors to prevent the bacon curling up, and lay in a single layer on a microwave roasting rack or large plate. Cover with a piece of absorbent kitchen paper to absorb the fat and stop it spitting. After cooking, remove the paper quickly to prevent it sticking to the bacon.

Biscuits (Cookies)

Q *My microwaved biscuits do not always turn out successfully. Can you tell me what I might be doing wrong?*

A Here are some possible causes of common problems:

- *One biscuit burns, others don't*: Cooker has a hot-spot—when cooking next batch of biscuits, arrange in a circle, leaving a space where biscuit burned previously.

- *Biscuits very chewy*: Cooking time too short—increase cooking time by 30 seconds, test one biscuit, then repeat if necessary; mixture not suitable for cooking in a microwave; power level incorrect.
- *Biscuit tough*: Cooking time too long—decrease by about 1 minute; mixture not suitable for cooking in a microwave.

Bread

Q *Can I refresh bread in a microwave?*

A Yes. Wrap it in a clean tea-towel and cook on HIGH for 15–30 seconds, until slightly warm on the surface.

Q *I made some bread in the microwave which turned out well but was extremely dry when sliced. Can you tell me what went wrong?*

A The mixture was too dry so more liquid needs to be added next time and the cooking time decreased.

Q *Can I warm bread rolls in the microwave?*

A Yes, place four rolls in a wicker serving basket and cook on HIGH for 30–40 seconds.

Q *When I warm bread rolls in the microwave they come out like hard bullets. What am I doing wrong?*

A You are heating them for too long and drying them out.

Browning dish

Q *I've heard that browning dishes can be used to brown foods in a microwave, but what are they exactly?*

A A microwave browning dish is made from ceramic coated with a special material which absorbs microwave energy. It should be preheated without food on it, then when the surface becomes hot it can be used to sear both sides of foods such as chops or steaks.

Cakes

Q *Can you give me some guidelines on the preparation and cooking of cakes in a microwave?*

A
- Be guided by conventional rules about greasing and lining containers, but avoid flouring dishes as this produces an unpalatable coating on the cake. Plastic cake-making containers do not need greasing unless the mixture contains only a small amount of fat, but other containers should be greased and the base of larger containers lined with greaseproof paper.

- Use baking containers that are large enough to allow for the mixture rising during cooking. Containers should not be more than half full of uncooked mixture.
- Mixtures should be of a softer consistency than when baked conventionally. Add an extra 30 ml (2 tbsp) milk for each egg used.
- When cooking a number of small cakes, arrange them in a circle in the cooker about 5 cm (2 inches) apart.
- Most cakes benefit from being cooked on a roasting rack as this enables maximum penetration of the microwaves and ensures that the cake is cooked in the centre. This will not be necessary if your cooker has a shelf. (If you do not have a roasting rack, use an upturned soup bowl instead.) This is not necessary with small cakes.
- Even if your cooker has a turntable, it is advisable to turn cakes to ensure even cooking.
- Always undercook cakes rather than over-cook. They can be returned to the cooker for a few extra minutes, if necessary, but over-cooked cakes will be dry and this cannot be rectified.
- Remove cakes from the cooker at the end of the recommended cooking time, even if the mixture looks wet. Standing time will complete the baking process.
- Turn out the cake after it has been left to stand, and immediately peel away the paper to prevent it sticking. Fragile soft cakes should be turned out on to a tea-towel placed over a wire rack to prevent the rack cutting into the cake.

Q *A microwave recipe book I have specifies using a ring mould for making cakes. Why is this necessary, and what could I use as an alternative?*

A If the cake mixture is deep and in a large container, the centre of the cake will not cook. Ring moulds are ideal and ensure even, overall cooking. It is possible to improvise by placing a heavy glass tumbler in the centre of a round dish, then pouring the mixture around it.

Cakes and teabreads

Q *My cakes and teabreads are not always successful when cooked in a microwave. Can you give me some hints as to what I might be doing wrong?*

A Here are some common causes of disappointment and some possible reasons for them.

- *Uncooked circle of mixture on base of cake or teabread*: The bottom of a deep cake or teabread cooks the most slowly—cook cake standing on a roasting rack or upturned plate (return partly uncooked cakes to the cooker, inverted on to a plate, and cook on HIGH for 1–3 minutes. Be careful not to over-cook; you should remove the mixture as soon as it has set); oven setting incorrect.
- *One large patch of a cake or teabread burned*: Oven has a hot-spot—turn cakes frequently during cooking.
- *Burned patches throughout a cake or teabread*: Lumpy sugar added to the mixture—the lumps of sugar get very hot during cooking and result in burned patches; too much dried fruit added (dried fruit contains a high proportion of sugar and has the same effect as lumps of sugar. If using your own recipe, cut down on the amount of fruit. Alternatively, try washing the fruit before coating it in flour. This should cut down on very sticky surfaces); too much sugar in the cake mixture. If adapting your own cake or teabread recipe it may be unsuitable.
- *Cake or teabread is dry*: Not enough liquid added—mixtures should be more moist than conventional cakes so add an extra 30 ml (2 tbsp) milk for every egg used; cooking time too long; mixture should have been covered during cooking to help retain moisture.
- *Teabread dry at ends but moist in centre*: Cooking time too long—watch teabreads during cooking: the ends will cook much faster than the centre. When the centre rises, test to see if cooked; power level incorrect (some teabreads benefit from being cooked on a MEDIUM setting); dish not turned during cooking. If the teabread is rising unevenly, it means that it is cooking unevenly. Watch during cooking and turn if necessary.

Casseroles and stews

Q *I tried to cook my favourite beef casserole in the microwave. I was very disappointed as, when it was cooked, the meat was extremely tough and there was too much liquid. Can you explain this?*

A Conventionally cooked casseroles and stews depend on long, slow cooking to tenderise tough cuts of meat and to allow the flavours of the vegetables and herbs to combine. For this reason, there is little point in using the microwave for stews other than those with ingredients which do not need tenderising, such as most poultry and vegetable stews and best quality meats.

When adapting conventional casserole or stew recipes to the microwave, it is usually necessary to reduce the amount of liquid as there is less evaporation when microwaving because of the reduced cooking time. Start with about one quarter less liquid and add more during cooking if necessary. Herbs and spices do not have time to mellow, so use half the amount stated in conventional recipes.

Cheese

Q *When I cook recipes containing cheese in the microwave, the texture becomes tough and rubbery. How can I overcome this?*

A Care must be taken when cooking with cheese. Always add it just before the end of cooking. It will melt more evenly and quickly if grated rather than sliced.

Chocolate

Q *I've heard that chocolate can be melted in a microwave. Is this possible?*

A Yes. To melt chocolate, break it into small pieces, unless using chocolate chips, place in a small bowl and cook on LOW just until the chocolate is soft and glossy on top. Remove from the cooker and stir until melted. As a guide, 100 g (4 oz) chocolate takes about 4 minutes on LOW. The melting times vary according to the material and shape of container used, so it is advisable to check every minute during melting. Take care not to over-cook and do not melt on HIGH or the chocolate may scorch.

Cookies, see Biscuits

Covering

Q *Is it safe to use cling film (plastic wrap) in a microwave cooker?*

A At the time of going to press, it has been recommended by the Ministry of Agriculture, Fisheries and Food that cling film should not be used in microwave cooking, as it has been found that some of the plasticiser di-2-ethyhexledipate (DEHA), used to soften cling film, can migrate into the food during cooking. When a recipe suggests covering a dish, use a lid or plate.

Dishes

Q *How can I check to see if a dish is suitable or not for microwave cooking?*

A Half fill the dish with water and heat on HIGH for 1 minute. If the water is hot and the top of the dish cool, the microwaves are passing through the material well. If both water and dish are warm, the dish can be used safely but cooking will be less efficient and slower because microwaves are being trapped in the material. If the dish is hot and the water cool, virtually all the microwaves are being trapped in the material and the dish is not suitable for microwave cooking.

Q *Which dishes are not suitable for microwave cooking?*

A Metal reflects microwaves so metal dishes should not be used. Also avoid using glass or china decorated with metal. Metal produces arcing (seen as a flare of light) which can damage the magnetron inside the cooker. Remember, metal tags can cause this as well. See also below.

Q *Should I use certain shaped dishes for microwave cooking?*

A It is best to use round, straight-sided, large, shallow dishes because they transmit microwaves quickly and efficiently. Other shapes tend to allow a concentration of microwaves at the corners resulting in uneven cooking and possible burning of food. Where a specific size or shape of dish is recommended in a recipe, it is best to use it as timing and results may vary if a different dish is used.

Dried fruit

Q *I've heard you can use the microwave to plump up dried fruit quickly. Is this possible?*

A Yes. Place the fruit in a dish, cover with water and cook on HIGH for about 5 minutes until plump and soft. Stir, leave to stand for 5 minutes, then drain well.

Eggs

Q *Can you cook scrambled eggs in the microwave?*

A Yes, scrambled eggs are not only quick to prepare, but there's no messy saucepan to clean afterwards. Whisk the eggs, milk and butter together in a bowl and cook on HIGH for 3–5 minutes, whisking frequently.

Q *Is it true that you can't boil an egg in the microwave?*

A Yes, foods with a shell or skin, such as potatoes and apples, are best pricked with a fork or cocktail stick before cooking whole, to allow hot air to escape during cooking. It is not that easy to pierce the shell of an egg and the build-up of hot air under the shell will cause the egg to explode, so eggs are better boiled conventionally.

Q *Is is possible to poach an egg in the microwave?*

A Yes. Break the egg into a ramekin dish or tea cup. Prick the yolk with a cocktail stick or the point of a sharp knife, before cooking, to prevent it exploding. Cook on HIGH for 1 minute, then leave to stand for 1 minute to set.

Fish

Q *Can you give me some hints for cooking fish successfully in the microwave?*

A
- Fish cooks very quickly so take care not to let it over-cook. Shellfish is particularly critical. Take into account the standing time, as during this time the heat will equalise throughout the food and any uncooked areas of fish will be cooked.

- To prevent fish drying out, brush the skin with melted butter or margarine.
- Arrange small whole fish in a cartwheel, with tails towards the centre, for more even cooking.
- Slash the skin of whole fish in two or three places to prevent it bursting during cooking.
- Large fish should be cooked in a single layer and turned over once during cooking.
- Fillets of fish may be cooked flat or rolled up. Re-position once during cooking.
- Season fish with salt *after* cooking to prevent it toughening and drying out the flesh.

Q *How do I thaw frozen fish cutlets or fillets in the microwave?*

A Keep them in their original wrappings, which should first be slashed. Thaw on HIGH for 3–4 minutes per 450 g (1 lb).

Q *How do I cook whole fish, cutlets or fillets in the microwave?*

A Cook on HIGH for 4–5 minutes per 450 g (1 lb).

Fruit juice

Q *Is it true that if oranges or lemons are warmed in the microwave before squeezing, they will produce more juice?*

A Yes. Cook on HIGH for 30–60 seconds before squeezing.

Gelatine

Q *Is it possible to dissolve gelatine in the microwave?*

A For magic, trouble-free gelatine, leave the measured gelatine and liquid to swell for a few minutes, then place the bowl in the microwave and cook on HIGH for 30–50 seconds until dissolved, stirring frequently. Do not boil.

Golden syrup and honey

Q *Can I use the microwave to restore the texture of golden syrup or honey which has crystallised*

A Yes. Place the syrup or honey in a heatproof bowl and cook on HIGH for 1–2 minutes until the texture is restored. If the syrup or honey is in a glass jar, you could put it in the microwave without transferring it to a bowl, but you must remove any metal lids, and take care not to heat for longer than specified as glass jars are not heatproof.

Hazelnuts

Q *Is is possible to remove the skins and brown hazelnuts in the microwave?*

A Yes. Place the hazelnuts in a single layer on absorbent kitchen paper and cook on HIGH for 30 seconds. Rub off the skins, return to the cooker and continue cooking until just golden, stirring frequently.

Honey, see Golden syrup

Liver

Q *When I cooked liver in the microwave, it popped and splattered all over the cooker. Why?*

A Liver (and kidneys) has a thin membrane surrounding it. During cooking, pressure builds up under this skin and causes it to pop, allowing the hot air to escape. This skin should be removed and the offal pricked with a fork before cooking.

Meat

Q *I have little success when cooking meat in the microwave. Can you give me some hints as to what I might be doing wrong?*

A These general tips might help:

- Do not add salt directly to meat before cooking as this draws out moisture and toughens the outside.
- Start meat cooking with the fat side down and turn it halfway through cooking if more than 5 cm (2 inches) thick.
- Improve browning by microwaving meat in a roasting bag.
- Joints of meat cook more evenly if symmetrically shaped, such as when boned and rolled.
- Position joints of meat so that the thickest parts are pointing towards the edge of the dish.
- For even cooking, turn over large joints or cuts at least once during cooking.

- As large joints need 15–20 minutes standing time, cover them with foil to keep the heat in, and leave in a warm place.
- Arrange meatballs in a circle on a plate to ensure even cooking, and try to leave a space in the middle so that microwaves can penetrate from the inside as well as the outside of the ring of meatballs.

Pasta

Q *Can you tell me how to cook pasta successfully in the microwave?*

A Remove the pasta from the cooker when it is still slightly undercooked, otherwise it will become soggy. Cover and leave to stand in its cooking liquid for 5–10 minutes to allow cooking to be completed. The amount of standing time depends on the pasta shape. The same principle applies when cooking grains, such as rice and barley.

Q *When cooking pasta in the microwave I find that it takes a long time to cook. Are there any time-saving tips?*

A Yes. Boil the water first in a kettle before adding it to the pasta. This also applies to grains.

Poultry and game

Q *Can you give me some hints for cooking poultry and game successfully in the microwave?*

A
- Roasting bags are useful for cooking poultry without spattering. Use an elastic band to secure them, not metal twist ties which could cause arcing. Pierce the bags before cooking to allow steam to escape.
- Boned and rolled poultry cooks more evenly because the shape and thickness are consistent.
- Arrange portions of poultry so that the thinnest parts are pointing towards the centre of the dish.
- Salt toughens poultry and makes it dry out if added directly to the food without any liquid. It is best to add it after cooking to ensure even cooking.
- When cooking duck, spoon off the fat during cooking to prevent a pool forming and spattering occurring. Cover with a pierced roasting bag.

- Poultry and game are cooked when the juices run clear when a knife is inserted into the thickest part of the meat.

Preserves

Q *Can jars that are to be used for preserves be sterilised in the microwave cooker?*

A Yes. Quarter fill up to four jars with water. Arrange them in a circle in the cooker, then bring to the boil on HIGH. Wearing oven gloves, remove each jar as it is ready and pour out the water. Invert the jar on a clean tea-towel or absorbent kitchen paper and use as required.

Reheating

Q *When I reheat baked pastry foods in the microwave, they tend to become either very soggy or very tough. Why is this and how can I prevent it?*

A Reheating in a microwave is extremely quick and special attention must be paid when reheating pastry-based foods. Microwaves are attracted to the moist filling in pies and pastries so that the liquid will heat up very quickly. The steam produced by this is often absorbed into the pastry covering, making it less crisp than when reheated in a conventional oven. When reheating, place foods either on a microwave roasting rack, so that the air can circulate underneath, or on absorbent kitchen paper to absorb moisture during reheating. Pastry should only be reheated for the minimum amount of time or it will become tough. The outer pastry should feel just warm. The temperature of pastry and filling will equalise if given a few minutes' standing time.

Salt

Q *Should I add salt before or after microwave cooking?*

A Salt toughens and causes dehydration of meat and vegetables cooked in the microwave. Always salt vegetables after cooking, and do not add any to meat until late in the cooking time. Less salt is needed for vegetables cooked in the microwave because their natural salts are retained due to the small amount of water used.

Sauces

Q *What microwave setting should I use for cooking sauces which are thickened with egg?*

A They are best cooked on a LOW setting, as care is needed to prevent them from curdling.

Q *How can I make a successful sauce in the microwave?*

A Sauces are excellent cooked in the microwave and there is little risk of lumps forming or burning occurring. Simply put the milk, butter, flour, salt and pepper in a bowl and cook on HIGH for 3–5 minutes, whisking frequently.

Standing time

Q *What is 'standing time'?*

A This technique is often over-emphasised and only applies to certain foods, such as cakes and meat. Food continues to cook after being removed from the microwave cooker, or when the power is switched off, because of the transfer of heat within the food. Some foods are therefore removed from the cooker before completely cooked, and cooking continues during standing time.

Sugar

Q *Is it possible to restore the texture of hardened sugar in the microwave?*

A Yes. To soften the sugar, leave it in its original wrappings and cook on HIGH for 30–40 seconds.

Vegetables

Q *I cannot master the skill of cooking vegetables in the microwave. Can you help?*

A Follow these basic guidelines for greater success.

- Cut vegetables into uniformly-sized pieces so that they cook evenly.
- Always pierce the skin of whole vegetables, such as potatoes, to prevent them bursting.
- For even cooking, arrange vegetables, such as cauliflower and broccoli florets, with the thickest part towards the edge of the dish.
- Turn large vegetables, such as potatoes and whole cauliflower, once during cooking, so that they cook evenly.

Q *What is the best way to cook frozen vegetables in the microwave?*

A Small frozen vegetables, such as peas, sweetcorn kernels and mixed vegetables, can be cooked in their plastic packets because the melting ice within the packet produces sufficient moisture for cooking. Slit the top of the packet and shake it about halfway through the cooking to distribute the heat evenly.

MILK

Q *When I boil milk in a saucepan it sticks to the bottom of the pan and makes it difficult to clean. Can I prevent this?*

A Before using a pan to heat milk, rinse it out with cold water. This will make it easier to clean afterwards.

N

NUTS

Q *How do I tell if nuts are fresh?*

A To judge the freshness of nuts in the shell, shake them. If the kernels inside rattle, it is an indication that the nuts are old and dried up.

Q *What is the best way to store an opened packet of nuts to keep them fresh?*

A Once you have opened a packet of nuts, keep them in the refrigerator. Re-seal the pack with a twist tie or keep in a small airtight container.

Almonds

Q *What is the best way to remove the skin of almonds?*

A Blanch the almonds quickly by pouring boiling water over them and leaving them for 2 minutes. Drain and drop into cold water. Rub the skins off with your fingers. Almonds stay juicier if not blanched, so don't do it until just before you need them.

Q *How do I sliver almonds?*

A Place them on a chopping board immediately after blanching and cut them into strips while they are still damp.

Chestnuts

Q *What quantity of chestnuts will I have once I have peeled 450 g (1 lb).*

A As a general rule, 450 g (1 lb) fresh chestnuts will yield about 350 g (12 oz) peeled nuts.

Q *Can I substitute canned or dried chestnuts for fresh ones in a recipe?*

A Yes, you can use dried or canned chestnuts (whole and unsweetened) instead of cooked fresh ones. Dried nuts should be soaked overnight and then treated the same as fresh chestnuts. 225 g (8 oz) dried chestnuts will yield about 450 g (1 lb) when cooked.

Q *Is there an easy way to peel chestnuts?*

A The best way is to make a tiny slit in the skin near the pointed end of each chestnut, then cover them with boiling water and leave for 5 minutes. Remove from the water, one at a time, and peel off the thick outer and thin inner skins while the nuts are still warm.

Hazelnuts

Q *What is the best way to remove the skin from hazelnuts?*

A Unlike almonds, blanching will not help to skin hazelnuts. Instead, grill hazelnuts until the skins split. (Watch and turn them often as they burn easily.) Place the nuts in a plastic bag and rub them against each other until the skins come off.

OFFAL

Kidneys

Q *Is there an easy way to remove cores from kidneys?*

A Yes. Simply halve the kidneys lengthways and snip out the cores with kitchen scissors.

Q *How many kidneys should I allow per serving?*

A Allow three per person for a main course and two per person for a breakfast or light dish.

Liver

Q *When I cook liver it always seems tough. What can I do to keep it tender?*

A Take care not to over-cook it. Steeping it in milk for 1 hour before cooking will help to make it tender.

Sweetbreads

Q *How do you prepare sweetbreads?*

A Soak for 2 hours in cold water to remove any blood, changing the water several times. Boil the sweetbreads for 10–15 minutes in plenty of water, drain, rinse in cold water and then remove the skin and any blood vessels. Use as required.

OVEN TEMPERATURES

Q *Some of my old cookery books don't give exact oven temperatures. Can you give me a guide as to what temperature I should set my oven?*

A The chart overleaf gives all the oven temperature conversions.

O

OVEN TEMPERATURES

°C	°F	Gas Mark	Description
110	225	$\frac{1}{4}$	Very Cool
130	250	$\frac{1}{2}$	
140	275	1	Cool
150	300	2	
170	325	3	Moderate
180	350	4	
190	375	5	Fairly Hot
200	400	6	
220	425	7	Hot
230	450	8	
240	475	9	Very Hot

P

PANCAKES (CREPES)

Q What are the basic ingredients quantities for pancake batter?

A 100 g (4 oz) flour, 1 egg, 300 ml ($\frac{1}{2}$ pint) milk and water mixed, and 1.25 ml ($\frac{1}{4}$ level tsp) salt. (Makes about eight pancakes.)

Q Why do my pancakes always stick to the pan?

A • Perhaps the pan was not seasoned before use. To help pancakes slide out of the pan easily, make sure your new cast iron or aluminium frying pan is seasoned properly first. To do this, pour some vegetable oil and a little salt into the pan, leave for 24 hours, then remove. Wipe out the pan with absorbent kitchen paper. Obviously, this is unnecessary if you have non-stick or high-quality stainless steel pans.

- Keep a special pan just for pancakes. Never wash it, simply wipe the inside surface clean with absorbent kitchen paper. Non-stick pans are recommended.

Q *My pancakes are never very successful. What am I doing wrong?*

A The following hints may help.

- *Soggy pancakes*: Batter too thick; fat not hot enough in frying pan; under-cooked; too much batter used for each pancake.
- *Pancakes break easily*: Batter too thin; insufficient egg.
- *Pancakes difficult to roll or fold*: Batter too thick; pancakes too thick; over-cooked.

PASTA

Q *How much pasta should I allow per serving of fresh and dried pasta?*

A Serving quantities of fresh and dried pasta are exactly the same. This is because dried pasta is much lighter than fresh to begin with, but it almost trebles in weight when cooked. Allow 50–75 g (2–3 oz) per person as a starter; 100–175 g (4–6 oz) per person as a main course.

Q *Should I cook pasta with or without a lid on the pan?*

A Cook pasta without a lid on the pan to prevent it going soggy. It should be served *al dente*, that is it should still have some bite to it.

Q *How long should I cook fresh or dried pasta?*

A After the water has returned to the boil, cook

- fresh pasta for 2–3 minutes
- dried pasta for 8–12 minutes
- fresh, filled pasta for 8–10 minutes
- dried, filled pasta for 15–20 minutes.

Q *Is it possible to stop cooked pasta from sticking together?*

A To prevent it sticking, toss the drained pasta in oil or butter.

Adding oil to the cooking water won't help; the oil simply rises to the surface.

Spaghetti

Q *I don't like to break up spaghetti, but how can I cook it whole if I don't have a large saucepan?*

A There is no need to break up long spaghetti to fit the pan. Just poke one end into the boiling water and coil it round as it softens until it is all under the water.

PASTRY

Ingredients

Q *What are the ingredients quantities for basic and rich shortcrust pastry?*

A For basic shortcrust pastry, you should use half as much fat as flour. For example, with 225 g (8 oz) plain flour, use a pinch of salt, 50 g (2 oz) butter or block margarine and 50 g (2 oz) lard, and about 60 ml (4 tbsp) ice-cold water.

For rich shortcrust pastry, increase the amount of fat to three quarters that of flour. The fat used should be butter and you should add 1 beaten egg yolk to the 45 ml (3 tbsp) ice-cold water needed.

Q *What are the basic ingredients quantities for suetcrust pastry?*

A 225 g (8 oz) self raising flour; 2.5 ml ($\frac{1}{2}$ level tsp) salt; 100 g (4 oz) shredded suet and about 120 ml (8 tbsp) ice-cold water.

Q *Which fats should I use for pastry making?*

A Use butter or block margarine at room temperature. For best results, combine with equal amounts of lard or white vegetable fat to make the pastry short. Choose the softer, quick-creaming margarine for quick-mix pastries using a specially formulated recipe.

Q *Have you a hint for making extra-light pastry?*

A For extra-light pastry, add a little lemon juice to the water when mixing.

Rolling out

Q Can you give me some hints for rolling out pastry?

A The following are general guidelines for rolling out pastry:

- Try not to add extra flour as this will toughen the pastry.
- Be careful not to stretch the pastry as this will cause it to shrink badly during baking.
- On a hot day, roll out pastry between two sheets of greaseproof paper.
- Do not over-handle the pastry.
- Roll the pastry in one direction only so that you do not stretch it.
- Rest the pastry in the refrigerator for about 20 minutes after you've rolled it out and used it to line or cover a dish.

Q What can I do with pastry that's too crumbly to roll out?

A Make it into a crumble topping. Break it up with a fork and add grated cheese for a savoury dish and sugar for a pudding.

Baking

Q *What temperature do I cook pastry at?*

A The following is a general guide:

• Shortcrust	200–220°C	(400–425°F)	mark 6–7
• Puff/flaky	200–220°C	(400–425°F)	mark 6–7
• Hot-water crust	220°C	(425°F)	mark 7
reducing to	180°C	(350°F)	mark 4
• Choux	200°C	(400°F)	mark 6
• Phyllo (filo)	190°C	(375°F)	mark 5

Q *How can I get puff pastry to rise well during baking?*

A To get the optimum rise from flaky pastries, bake on a damp baking sheet.

What went wrong?

Q *I can't make pastry successfully. Can you give me some hints as to where I might be going wrong?*

A The following notes should help you discover what the problem is.

Shortcrust pastry

- *Hard and/or tough*: Insufficient fat (shortening); too much liquid; over-handling; cooking too slowly.
- *Crumbly, too short and hard to handle*: Too much fat; over-mixing; not enough liquid to bind fat and flour; self raising flour used.
- *Soggy inside*: Insufficient baking; filling too hot when covered by pastry; no steam vent made; too much liquid; too much sugar in contact with pastry.
- *Shrinkage during baking*: Pastry stretched during rolling and shaping; insufficient resting time—allow at least 20 minutes in the refrigerator.
- *Blistered crust*: Fat insufficiently rubbed in; water unevenly mixed in.

- *Flan case base risen during baking*: Self raising flour used; pastry not carefully pressed into tin to exclude air underneath; pastry not pricked with a fork to prevent air pockets, or not weighted down with baking beans or foil during baking.
- *Cooked cheese pastry tough and rubbery with a rough appearance*: Cheese grated too coarsely; cheese too fresh, causing it to stick together and disperse unevenly in mixing; baked in too hot an oven, causing the cheese to melt and bubble.
- *Cooked rich pastry has a speckled appearance*: Granulated sugar used; too much sugar used; baked in too hot an oven.

Suetcrust pastry

- *Hard and tough*: Insufficient baking powder used if plain flour is used; over-handled; too much water; baked in too hot an oven.
- *Small lumps of undissolved suet in cooked pastry*: Suet not shredded sufficiently finely; oven too hot.

Puff, flaky and rough puff pastry

- *Hard and tough*: Too much liquid; dough insufficiently kneaded; rolling in of fat done too heavily and for too long; not kept cool; too much flour used during rolling; oven too cool.
- *Poor volume, lacking in flakiness*: Fat too warm and blended with flour instead of remaining in layers; lemon juice omitted (lemon juice reacts with the gluten in the flour which makes the dough more pliable); insufficient resting between rolling; edges sealed with glaze; oven too cool.
- *Soggy in middle*: Under-baking; oven too hot; baked too high in oven.
- *Shrinkage during baking*: Pastry over-stretched during rolling; insufficient resting time(s)—at least 20 minutes in refrigerator for every rolling and folding; oven too cool.
- *Uneven rise*: Unevenly rolled or folded; fat unevenly distributed; sides not straight and corners not square during rolling out; edges not trimmed before use; insufficient resting between rollings or before baking; uneven oven temperature; too much glaze used, particularly on edges.

Hot-water crust pastry

- *Dry, crumbly and will not mould*: Insufficient fat; insufficient water; fat and water too cool when added to flour; dough cooled before kneading.
- *Crust burst after being filled or during baking*: Crust unevenly moulded or too thin in parts; careless handling.
- *Texture crumbly and doughy*: Self raising flour used.
- *Soggy layer of pastry inside pie*: Filling too moist; oven too hot; insufficient baking.

Choux pastry

- *Pastry too thin*: Ingredients incorrectly measured; water not boiling when flour added; insufficient beating.
- *Pastry too thick*: Ingredients incorrectly measured; liquid boiled too long and evaporated.
- *Cooked pastry close and heavy*: Insufficient beating (always add the beaten egg(s) a little at a time, beating thoroughly until the mixture is really lacy looking); oven too cool.
- *Eclairs badly cracked*: Oven too hot.

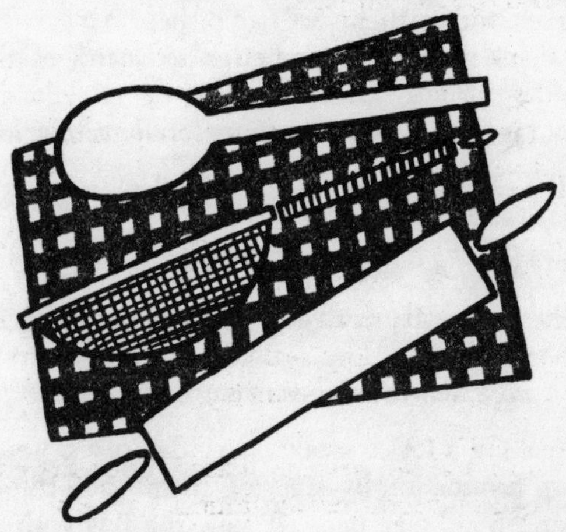

Flan cases (pie shells)

Q *Can you tell me how much pastry I need to make various sizes of flan.*

A The following chart is a guide to the quantity of pastry you will need.

Dish Size *Plain or Fluted Flan Ring*	**Pastry** *(Flour weight)*
15 cm (6 inch)	100 g (4 oz)
18 cm (7 inch)	150 g (5 oz)
20.5 cm (8 inch)	175 g (6 oz)
23 cm (9 inch)	200 g (7 oz)

Loose-bottomed metal flan tins are shallower than flan rings, china dishes or sandwich tins and require less pastry (and filling) than indicated.

Q *How can you ensure the pastry will be crisp when baking a flan case.*

A Stand glass and earthenware flan dishes on a preheated metal baking sheet as this acts as a better conductor of heat.

Q *How can I prevent a pastry flan from over-browning at the edges?*

A Cover the edges with thin strips of foil.

Q *How can I avoid a soggy base to a flan?*

A Brush the raw pastry with egg white before baking.

Q *Is there a quick way to bake small pastry flan cases?*

A When making a lot of small pastry flan cases, you can really speed up production by stacking them up in threes or fours for baking blind (see page 9). Line the tins with pastry and chill well, then stack them one on top of the other, lining only the top one with foil and baking beans.

Q *What is the neatest way to trim an uncooked pastry flan case?*

A Don't trim round the edge with a knife. The neatest way is to roll a rolling pin across the top. The pastry will fall away.

Q *How do I remove a cooked flan from a loose-bottomed tin without burning myself?*

A Place it on a jam jar and slip the metal ring down and away.

Q *What is the best way of transferring a cooked flan to a serving plate?*

A When using a flan ring, place it on an upturned baking sheet for baking so that you can just slide it off when cooked.

Q *Is it possible to repair a cracked pastry flan case?*

A Yes. Brush all over the cracks with beaten egg white. Return to the oven for a few minutes until the egg white has sealed the cracks.

PIPING BAG

Q *I don't have a piping bag; can I make one?*

A Make an emergency piping bag by snipping off the corner of a small (not gusseted) plastic bag. Insert nozzle and secure with sticky tape.

Q *What is the best way to fill a piping bag with cream or butter cream?*

A Place the bag, nozzle down, in a jug. Fold some of the piping bag back over the rim of the jug. This leaves both hands free to fill the bag.

POULTRY

Q *How can I tell if poultry is cooked?*

A Push a skewer into the thickest part, usually the thigh. If the juices run clear (not pink), the poultry is cooked.

Chicken

Q *At what temperature and for how long should I roast chicken?*

A Roast at 200°C (400°F) mark 6, allowing 20 minutes per 450 g (1 lb), plus 20 minutes.

Q *How many people will various sizes of chicken serve?*

A
- A 1.4 kg (3 lb) chicken will serve 4
- A 1.8 kg (4 lb) chicken will serve 4–5
- A 2 kg (4½ lb) chicken will serve 5–6
- A 2.4 kg (5¼ lb) chicken will serve 6–8

Q *I want to make a recipe using cold chicken. How much meat will a whole cooked chicken give me?*

A A 1.4 kg (3 lb) cooked chicken will yield 350 g (12 oz) meat. A 2 kg (4½ lb) chicken will yield 700 g (1½ lb) meat.

Duck

Q *When buying duck, how much should I allow per person?*

A Allow at least 450 g (1 lb) per person. Never buy a duck weighing less than 1.4 kg (3 lb) as the proportion of bone will be too high. As a guide, a 2.3 kg (5 lb) duck will serve four people and two 1.8 kg (4 lb) ducks will serve six people.

Q *What is the best way to roast duck?*

A Duck is very fatty, so prick the skin all over with a skewer or fork so that the fat drains off during roasting, and rub the skin with salt. Place the duck on a trivet in a roasting tin.

Q *At what temperature and for how long should I roast duck?*

A Roast at 180°C (350°F) mark 4, allowing 30 minutes per 450 g (1 lb).

Turkey

Q *How many people will a turkey serve?*

A
- A 3.6–5 kg (8–11 lb) turkey will serve 10–15
- A 5–6·8 kg (11–15 lb) turkey will serve 15–20
- A 6.8–9 kg (15–20 lb) turkey will serve 20–30

Q *At what temperature and for how long should I roast turkey?*

A Roast at 180°C (350°F) mark 4, allowing 20 minutes per 450 g (1 lb), plus 20 minutes.

PRESERVES

Pots and pans

Q *Can I use my brass preserving pan for making jam and pickles?*

A Brass preserving pans and unlined copper pans are no longer recommended for preserving as the acid in the food will attack the metal. Aluminium preserving pans are now recommended.

Q *I am frightened of pouring hot preserves into the jars in case they crack. What should I do?*

A The jars won't crack if you stand them on a wet cloth on top of a wooden board when you pour in the hot preserve.

Q *I can't remove the screw-bands of my stored preserves. Can you help me?*

A If the screw-bands are rusted on, try pouring hot water on to loosen them. If stubborn, put a few drops of oil round the top and bottom of each screw-band and leave for a day or two for the oil to penetrate before trying again.

Setting point

Q *How do I tell when my cooked preserve is at setting point?*

A Use one of the following methods:

- *Thermometer*: Put a sugar thermometer, first into hot water, and then submerge it in the preserve. When the reading is 105°C (221°F) a set should be obtained.
- *Flake*: Dip a clean wooden spoon into the boiling preserve. Let the preserve on the spoon cool a little, then let it drop back into the pan. If the drops run together, forming a 'flake', it is ready.
- *Plate*: Pour a little of the preserve on to a small, cold plate and leave it to cool. If it wrinkles when a finger is pushed gently through it, setting point has been reached.

What went wrong?

Q *When I make preserves they do not always turn out successfully. Can you tell me what I might be doing wrong?*

A The following points may be of help.

- *Syrup consistency*: Over-ripe fruit; too short or too long boiling after addition of sugar; unbalanced recipe (deficiency of pectin or acid or too high a proportion of sugar); inaccurate weighing.
- *Fermented (berry) preserve*: Insufficient sugar; too high a yield from sugar used; insufficient boiling; warm storage after opening the jar.
- *Sugar crystals*: Under-boiling; too little acid.
- *Needle crystals or a solid mass*: Over-boiling; too much acid; fruit or extract not sufficiently reduced before adding sugar.
- *Dull, brownish colour or cloudy*: Poor fruit; over-cooking after the addition of sugar; failure to remove scum; storage too warm or too light.
- *Air bubbles throughout*: Poured into jars too slowly (especially jelly); allowed to cool too much before potting.
- *Tough skins or peel (especially blackcurrant)*: Insufficient

simmering with water to soften skins before the addition of sugar.

- *Fruit or peel risen in jar*: Preserve not allowed to cool—to about 76°C (170°F)—before potting; jars too hot.
- *Weeping jelly*: Too much acid in fruit or in recipe.
- *Cloudy jelly*: Dirty fruit; jelly bag mesh not sufficiently close; jelly bag squeezed to hasten process.

Q *What do I do if my preserve develops mould?*

A Mould growth usually occurs because the preserve has not been covered with a wax disc while still hot. Alternatively, the pots may have been stored in a place where they picked up bacteria and were not cleaned properly. Other possible causes are insufficient evaporation of water while the fruit is being cooked before sugar is added and/or too short a boiling time after the sugar is added. It is important not to eat a preserve that has mould growth on it as it produces toxins. Throw away the whole jar if you find any mould on the top surface.

Bottling (canning)

Q *I've never bottled fruits before, can you give me some hints to ensure success?*

A
- The bottles must be scrupulously clean.
- The rubber rings should be examined carefully for flaws. Good, soft rubber rings should always be used. They are best soaked in warm water for 15 minutes, then dipped in boiling water before use.
- Bottle rims and bottle lids should be examined and those with chips rejected.
- A false bottom should always be placed in the pan for water bath and pressure cooker methods, otherwise some bottles may crack.
- When using screw-band jars, the screw-bands must not be tight when the jars are placed in the steriliser but should be tightened immediately after processing. For oven methods, do not put the screw-band on whilst processing.
- Care should be taken that the processing times and temperatures given are adhered to. If the water is too hot, the contents of the bottles will go mushy and become un-

sightly; the appearance will also be spoiled by the fruit rising in the bottles.

- The screw-bands or clips should be left on until the bottles are quite cold.
- Bottles should never be put in to the oven with bands screwed on tightly, as they may be difficult to remove later. It is a good plan to take them off when the bottles are cold, dry well, and smear inside with a little oil. Each band can then be put back loosely on the same bottle.

Q *I've bottled some fruits but they don't look as good as those you can buy. Can you tell me what I have done wrong?*

A The following points may help you discover your mistake:

- *Poor colour of fruit*: Fruit over-ripe or under-ripe; slow preparation; poor processing method; fruit over-processed; failure to store bottled fruit in a dark, cool place.
- *Discoloration of fruit at top of jar*: Delayed preparation (eg apples); fruit not covered by liquid; jars not covered with water in water bath; fruit under-processed.
- *Fruit risen in jar*: Over-ripe fruit; failure to pack tightly;

over-processed or too rapidly processed. (Fruit is more likely to rise when packed in syrup than when water is used. A slight rise is not considered a fault in syrup packs.)

- *Cloudy fluid*: Fruit over-ripe; fruit dirty; syrup not strained before use; fruit over-processed.
- *Air bubbles in jar*: Fruit packed too tightly; failure to shake out bubbles when filling bottle with liquid.

Jam

Q *Can you give me some hints for making jam successfully?*

A
- Firm-ripe, fresh fruit should be used; over-ripe fruit should be avoided.
- Fruit that needs softening should be allowed to simmer gently before the sugar is added.
- To get a well-set jam it is necessary to have pectin, acid and sugar present in the correct proportions.
- Sugar should not be added until the fruit is well cooked and broken down. After sugar has been added the jam should be boiled *rapidly* until setting point is reached.
- To prevent fruit rising in the jars, especially strawberries and cherries, the jam should be allowed to cool slightly in the pan and then stirred before filling the jars.
- Over-boiling with sugar darkens the colour, spoils the flavour and may cause a sticky jam.
- If airtight covers are used, they should be scrupulously clean and should be placed on the jars immediately after filling.
- Jam should be stored in a dry, dark, cool, ventilated cupboard.

Q *What can I do with jam that has not set?*

A
- Try tipping it back into the pan and re-boiling with extra lemon juice, or add a commercial pectin, following the manufacturer's instructions.
- Use it as a fruit sauce for hot puddings or ice cream.

Q *Why has my jam crystallised?*

A Crystallisation is usually caused by lack of enough acid, or by under- or over-boiling the jam after the sugar has been added.

Q *What do I do if there's scum on top of my jam and how do I remove it?*

A This is usual when making jam, but don't be tempted to remove the scum until the jam is made—continuous skimming is wasteful and unnecessary. Adding a knob of butter, when you add the sugar, helps to reduce the amount of scum. Remove the scum by skimming the surface with a slotted spoon.

Q *Why has my jam shrunk in its jar?*

A Shrinkage of jam in jars is caused by inadequate covering or failure to store the jam in a cool, dark, dry place.

Q *My jam has developed bubbles in it. Can I still eat it?*

A Bubbles in jam indicate fermentation, which is usually because not enough sugar has been used, or because the jam was not reduced sufficiently. Fermented jam can be boiled up again and re-potted but should only be used for cooking.

Jam and marmalade

Q *Can you suggest any different flavourings I could add to my jams and marmalades?*

A
- Add 15 ml (1 level tbsp) crushed coriander seeds, tied in a muslin (cheesecloth) bag, to the simmering peel to emphasise the flavour of the oranges in marmalade.
- Use 1–2 pieces of bruised root ginger (crushed with a rolling pin) in the same way. You can follow it up with the addition of chopped crystallised ginger at the very end.
- Stir 15 ml (1 tbsp) dark treacle into the marmalade with the sugar for a slightly bitter taste and rich dark colour.
- Stir in a miniature bottle of Cointreau, Armagnac, or Calvados (especially good with apple type preserves).
- Crack a few apricot stones and return one or two of the inner kernels to fresh apricots, when cooking, to emphasise the flavour.

Jelly

Q *Can you give me some hints on how to make jellies successfully?*

A
- The fruit should simmer gently and be thoroughly broken up before it is strained.
- The pulp should be allowed to strain without squeezing if a clear jelly is required, but the juice should not be left for more than 1 day before the jelly is finished.
- To get a well-set jelly it is necessary to have pectin, acid and sugar present in the correct proportions.
- Generally speaking, the sugar should not be added to the strained juice until it has been brought to boiling point, and if it seems rather thin it is advisable to reduce further before adding the sugar. With pale juices, such as apple and gooseberry, it is perhaps better, from the point of view of colour only, to add the sugar when the juice is cold. The longer heating of the juice and sugar together makes the resulting jelly a deeper colour.
- After the sugar has been added, the jelly should be skimmed and poured into jars as quickly as possible.
- Waxed circles should be placed on top of the hot jelly immediately the jars are filled.
- The jars should not be tilted until the jelly has set.

Mincemeat

Q *Why has my mincemeat fermented?*

A This is usually marked by oozing out of the jars, and is generally caused by lack of care in preparation, eg mixing on a floury board, insufficient sugar, not enough lemon juice, unsuitable apples, or poor storage conditions. Possibly the most frequent cause is using insufficient sugar, or the inclusion in the mixture of too large a proportion of soft sweet or semi-sweet apples instead of a measured quantity of hard sour apples. It is important not to introduce excess flour, but small amounts of flour, such as are contained in packaged suet, do not seem to cause trouble. Cover and store the mincemeat in a cool dry place. If fermentation has occurred, boil the mincemeat in a saucepan, and re-pot in sterilised jars. This will spoil the natural appearance, but will not affect the taste of the finished produce.

Fermentation should not, however, be confused with the juiciness which develops once the sugar has begun to form a syrup. This syrupy condition is a sign that the mincemeat is maturing well.

Pickles and chutneys

Q *Why have the top layers of my pickled vegetables and fruit turned black and why are they no longer covered with vinegar?*

A The cover must have been poor, allowing evaporation to take place, and/or the pickles were insufficiently covered with vinegar. Allow at least 1 cm ($\frac{1}{2}$ inch) vinegar or vinegar syrup above the top of all the fruit/vegetables as there is always slight evaporation of the vinegar in pickling.

Q *There is mould growing on top of my pickles and chutneys. What have I done wrong?*

A Somehow, air has got into the jars or the vinegar has been diluted too much to create complete preservation (perhaps due to insufficient brining or too much water being added to the vinegar), or the jars have been stored in a damp atmosphere.

Q *Why do I get yellow spots on my pickled onions?*

A There is nothing wrong with your onions and they are not harmful in any way. Yellow spots are probably due to the onions being drawn from the ground before they had become dormant. Try brining the onions for 3–4 days before pickling instead of the more usual short brining time.

Q *Why have my chutneys and pickles shrunk badly with a tough layer on top?*

A This is probably due to incorrect seals. The covers are either not airtight or not vinegar-proof, both of which are essential when using vinegar.

PUDDINGS, STEAMED, see STEAMED PUDDINGS

PULSES

Q *Sometimes I forget to soak dried beans overnight. Is there a quicker way to prepare them?*

A Yes, the soaking time of dried beans can be shortened by bringing them to the boil in a pan of water, then steeping them for 1–2 hours off the heat. Drain and cook in fresh water.

Q *What size can of beans should I use to substitute 100 g (4 oz) dried beans?*

A Use a 400 g (14 oz) can.

Q *How do I stop pulses from cracking and becoming mushy during cooking?*

A Add a pinch of baking powder to the water.

Q *How do I stop pulses becoming tough during cooking?*

A Add salt at the end of the cooking time, not at the beginning.

Q *Is it true that kidney beans can be poisonous?*

A All legumes, once they have been dried, contain a variety of toxic substances, most of which are present in insignificant amounts. The toxins that can be a hazard are the haemagglutinins which occur in high concentrations in kidney beans and soya beans. The haemagglutinins are virtually eliminated by cooking—if the pulses are cooked for at least 10 minutes in boiling water they are completely safe to eat.

You should do this before adding beans to *any* dish or if you are preparing them for a salad. If you are using a slow cooker remember that food cooked in these never reaches 100°C (212°F) so, again, it is essential to boil the beans for 10 minutes before adding them to the other ingredients. The only exception is canned beans—the canning process involves very high temperatures which destroy the toxins and the beans can be safely eaten.

Fresh beans, peas and sprouted beans do not contain high levels of toxins and therefore can be eaten raw.

Q *Can you tell me how long to cook the various types of pulses?*

A Refer to the following chart.

COOKING TIMES FOR PULSES

Type	Boiling Time *(approx)*	Pressure Cooking **
Aduki beans	30 minutes	15 minutes
Black beans	1 hour	20 minutes
Black-eye beans	45 minutes	12 minutes
Butter beans	50 minutes	17 minutes
Cannellini beans	1½ hours	25 minutes
Chick-peas and peas	1½ hours	20 minutes
Flageolet beans	1¼ hours	14 minutes
Haricot beans	1¼ hours	18 minutes
Lentils	1 hour	15 minutes
Mung beans	30 minutes	10 minutes
Red kidney beans*	50 minutes	17 minutes
Soya beans*	1½ hours	25 minutes
Split peas	45 minutes	15 minutes

* Never eat raw. Kidney and Soya must be soaked and boiled for at least 10 minutes before cooking until tender. Never cook the beans in an electric casserole (slow cooker) unless they have first been boiled for 10 minutes.

** 100 g (4 oz) beans requires 600 ml (1 pint) water. Bring to the boil in an open pan, skim, then cook at HIGH (15 lb) pressure.

Q *When a recipe needs a certain quantity of cooked beans, how do I know how many raw beans to cook?*

A Beans double in weight once cooked, so for a recipe needing 225 g (8 oz) cooked beans you should cook 100 g (4 oz) dried beans.

R

RECIPE QUANTITIES

Q *If I want to double the quantities of a recipe, do I simply double all the ingredients and the cooking time?*

A No. When doubling the quantities in a recipe, you don't necessarily need to double the amount of seasoning needed, or the time the dish takes to cook. Use the given amount of seasoning and check the taste before adjusting it. If the dish is not cooked by the time stated, continue cooking, testing from time to time, until it is cooked.

RICE

Q *By how much is a quantity of rice increased during cooking?*

A Raw rice trebles in weight during cooking.

Q *How do I keep rice white?*

A Add a few drops of fresh lemon juice to the boiling water.

Q *How much rice should I allow per person?*

A Allow 50 g (2 oz) raw rice per person.

Q *Can I cook rice in advance and then reheat it?*

A Rice can be cooked up to 3 days in advance and stored in a covered container in the refrigerator. To reheat, place in a roasting tin, dot with butter, cover with kitchen foil and place in a preheated oven at 180°C (350°F) mark 4 for 30–40 minutes. Fork through after 15 minutes.

ROASTING

Meat

Q *At what temperature, and for how long, should I roast joints of meat?*

A The process known as 'oven roasting' is in fact 'baking'. The oven should be preheated to 180°C (350°F) mark 4. This low temperature will produce succulent meat with less shrinkage. The traditional high-temperature cooking is only suitable for top-quality meat.

Weigh the joint as it is to be cooked (ie on the bone or boned and rolled or stuffed, as appropriate). Put in a shallow roasting tin, preferably on a grid. Cook for the time shown below:

- *Beef* (rare) 15 minutes per 450 g (1 lb) plus 15 minutes (medium-rare) 20 minutes per 450 g (1 lb) plus 20 minutes (well done) 25 minutes per 450 g (1 lb) plus 25 minutes
- *Lamb* (medium) 25 minutes per 450 g (1 lb) plus 25 minutes (well done) 30 minutes per 450 g (1 lb) plus 30 minutes
- *Pork* 30 minutes per 450 g (1 lb) plus 30 minutes
- *Veal* 25 minutes per 450 g (1 lb) plus 25 minutes

These roasting times are only meant as a guide. A long, thin piece of meat will take proportionately less time to cook than a thick, rolled piece weighing the same.

Q *Should I add fat to meat when roasting or not?*

A Cuts of meat with a natural layer of fat are self-basting; other meats will require dripping or lard.

Poultry, see page 99.

S

SALAD (see also FRENCH DRESSING)

Q *How do I stop salad going soggy?*

A Only dress a salad *just* before serving, taking care not to use too much dressing.

Q *How much French dressing should I use?*

A About 60 ml (4 tbsp) French dressing is enough for about 450 g (1 lb) salad to serve four people, but the important thing is not to drown the salad in dressing. There should be just enough to coat the ingredients without leaving a pool in the bottom of the bowl.

SALT

Q *How do I prevent salt going damp?*

A Keep a few grains of rice in the jar.

Q *Help! What can I do if I add too much salt to a soup or stew?*

A Add a peeled potato and boil for a few minutes, then remove it. The potato will absorb some of the salt.

SANDWICHES

Q *I want to make a large quantity of sandwiches. Can you give me a guide as to how many slices of bread there are in a loaf and how much butter I will need?*

A
- A sandwich loaf weighing 800 g ($1\frac{3}{4}$ lb) yields 22 slices and requires 100 g (4 oz) creamed butter or margarine.
- An unsliced bloomer loaf yields about 16 slices and requires 100 g (4 oz) creamed butter or margarine.
- A French stick 50 cm (20 inches) long yields 20 slices or

five chunks and requires about 175 g (6 oz) creamed butter or margarine.

- 24 bread rolls require 200 g (7 oz) creamed butter or margarine.

Q *How do you make rolled sandwiches for cocktail or drinks parties?*

A Remove the crusts and roll the slices of bread out with a rolling pin. Spread with butter and roll up around ham, (add a little mustard), smoked salmon or asparagus tips. They will stay tightly closed.

Q *I often have to make large quantities of sandwiches. Do you know any time-saving short-cuts?*

A
- When making mounds of sandwiches, cream the butter in an electric mixer, then combine it with the filling. This cuts the amount of spreading you have to do by half.
- If you haven't got a sliced loaf and you want to make a lot of sandwiches, cut the loaf lengthways. This gives the same number of sandwiches but doesn't involve so much spreading.

SAUCES

Ingredients

Q *What are the basic ingredients quantities for the different thicknesses of sauces?*

A Here are the basic sauce quantities:

- *Pouring consistency*: 25 g (1 oz) flour, 25 g (1 oz) butter or margarine, 600 ml (1 pint) liquid such as milk.
- *Coating*: 50 g (2 oz) flour, 50 g (2 oz) butter or margarine, 600 ml (1 pint) liquid.
- *Binding (panada)*: 100 g (4 oz) flour, 100 g (4 oz) butter or margarine, 600 ml (1 pint) liquid.

Q *How can I enhance the flavour of a cheese sauce?*

A Add a little French mustard. Alternatively, if you like the speckled appearance, add a whole grain mustard of your choice.

Q *What makes a white sauce glossy?*

A Add a spoonful or so of cream at the last minute—but be careful not to re-boil the sauce or it could separate.

What went wrong?

Q *Why do my sauces sometimes thicken and then become thin during cooking?*

A If a sauce becomes thin during cooking, it usually means it has been cooked too long, causing a chemical change to take place.

Q *My sauce has gone lumpy—how do I rectify it?*

A Try whizzing it in a blender or food processor, then return it to the saucepan and bring to the boil, stirring all the time. Alternatively, you can strain the lumpy sauce through a sieve.

Q *My sauces always go lumpy. Do you know of a quick, foolproof way to make a sauce?*

A Try using the all-in-one method. Forget the old laborious making of a roux for white sauce—simply whisk all the ingredients in the saucepan over a medium heat until the sauce thickens and comes to the boil. Use a good quality balloon whisk. Simmer to cook as usual.

Q *How do I prevent a skin forming on a sauce if I make it in advance?*

A If you're making a sweet or savoury sauce in advance and want to prevent a skin forming, you can pour a little cold milk over the top or dot with extra butter, then beat it in when you reheat it. Alternatively, a piece of damp greaseproof paper pressed down on to the surface of the sauce will stop a skin forming. (See also CUSTARD, page 29.)

SCONES

Ingredients

Q *What are the basic ingredients quantities for a batch of scones?*

A 225 g (8 oz) plain flour, 20 ml (4 level tsp) baking powder (or 225 g/8 oz self raising flour plus 5 ml/1 level tsp baking powder), 2.5 ml ($\frac{1}{2}$ level tsp) salt, 40–50 g ($1\frac{1}{2}$–2 oz) butter or block margarine and 150 ml ($\frac{1}{4}$ pint) milk. (Makes 8–12 scones.)

What went wrong?

Q *Can you give me any hints as to why I never make scones successfully?*

A The following are common problems and possible causes.

- *Heavy and badly risen*: insufficient raising (leavening) agent; heavy handling, especially during the kneading; insufficient liquid; oven too cool or the position for baking too low in the oven.
- *Scones spread and lose their shape*: Slack dough, caused by too much liquid used to make the dough; too heavily greased tin (the fat melts on heating in the oven and 'pulls out'. the soft dough before it has enough time to set); incorrect kneading (especially of the scraps for the second rolling) or twisting the cutter round as the scones were stamped out (such scones are oval instead of round when cooked).

- *Very rough surface*: insufficient or badly done kneading; rough handling when transferring to the baking sheet.

Griddle scones

Q *I can't make griddle scones successfully. Can you give me some hints?*

A The following hints may tell you where you are going wrong.
- *Sticking to griddle*: Griddle insufficiently greased, or dirty.
- *Spreading*: Batter too thin (it should only just pour from the spoon).
- *Pale and leathery*: Griddle too cool.
- *Over-browned and hard*: Griddle too hot.

SEAFOOD, see Fish

SOUFFLES

Q *What is the best way to prepare a soufflé dish?*

A To prepare a soufflé dish, cut a double length of greaseproof paper that will extend about 5 cm (2 inches) above the rim of the dish. Draw the paper tightly around the outside of the dish and secure with two or three paper clips. Cool the dish in the refrigerator before adding the mixture so that the soufflé setting is accelerated.

Q *Can you give me some hints for making a perfectly baked soufflé?*

A
- Always use a greased straight-sided dish to ensure even rising.
- Place the soufflé in a preheated oven and preheat a baking sheet in the oven to place the soufflé dish on.
- Don't slam the oven door!

Q *When I make a soufflé during a dinner party, how do I avoid disturbing my guests with the deafening noise of the electric mixer?*

A
- The soufflé can be prepared ahead of the dinner party. Fill the dish (or dishes) and leave in the refrigerator for up to 2 hours.

- Freeze the prepared soufflé, then cook from frozen, increasing the cooking time by a quarter.

Q *How full should I fill a soufflé dish?*

A Only fill three-quarters full to allow room for rising.

SOUP

Q *How much soup should I allow per serving?*

A Allow 150–200 ml (5–7 fl oz) per person for a starter and 225–300 ml (8–10 fl oz) for a main dish soup.

SOURDOUGH

Q *What is a sourdough starter?*

A A sourdough starter is used to make sourdough bread. It comprises 15 g (½ oz) dried (active dry) yeast, 5 ml (1 level tsp) caster sugar, 450 ml (¾ pint) tepid water and 225 g (8 oz) strong white (bread) flour. It should be prepared at least three days in advance and stored in the refrigerator until required. If you make sourdough bread often, the advantage of a starter is that it can be replenished and used over and over again so that you need never buy more yeast.

To make the starter, sprinkle the yeast and sugar on to 150 ml ($\frac{1}{4}$ pint) of the water and leave until frothy. Mix in the remaining water and flour. Cover and leave in a warm place for 48 hours, stirring occasionally, until it has risen and bubbled, then separated. Stir well before using 225 ml (8 fl oz) starter to make two 900 g (2 lb) loaves. Replenish the remaining starter by beating 100 g (4 oz) strong white flour with 225 ml (8 fl oz) tepid water until smooth. Stir this into the remaining 225 ml (8 fl oz) starter. Leave until the mixture begins to bubble, then cover loosely and refrigerate until required for the next batch of bread.

SPICES (see also HERBS AND SPICES)

Q *I don't have any mace. Can I replace it with another spice?*

A Mace and nutmeg are interchangeable as they come from the same plant. Mace is a little stronger.

Q *How can I bring out the full flavour of a spicy dish?*

A When cooking a dish which contains spices, herbs, onion or garlic, try to cook the dish the day before. The flavours will be twice as good on the second day as they will have had time to mellow and develop.

Q *Does it make any difference if I use ready-ground spices, or should I grind them myself?*

A Whole spices which you grind yourself will give a more pungent flavour than those which are ready-ground.

Q *Is chilli seasoning the same as chilli powder?*

A No, chilli seasoning contains other spices and is not as hot as chilli powder.

Q *Saffron is expensive; is there a substitute?*

A A small quantity of turmeric makes an adequate substitute for expensive saffron.

STEAMED PUDDINGS

Q *How do I stop my saucepan discolouring when I steam puddings?*

A Add a teaspoon of vinegar to the water.

Q *My steamed puddings are rarely successful. What am I doing wrong?*

A The following hints may help you.

- *Pudding heavy and soggy*: Mixture too wet; inadequate covering of pudding; water off boil; undercooking; filling too moist.
- *Pudding too dry*: Mixture too dry; over-cooking.
- *Pudding breaks and sticks to bowl when turned out*: Bowl insufficiently greased; pudding not left to stand for 3–4 minutes before turning out; undercooking.

STOCK

Q *If I haven't time to make stock, can I keep the bones for using later?*

A Yes, you can store bones in a plastic bag in the freezer until you have more time.

Q *I like to make a large quantity of stock and then freeze it, but it takes up a lot of space in the freezer. Can you suggest how I can save freezer space?*

A Reduce stock to a concentrated form before freezing. This is done by boiling rapidly in an uncovered pan to evaporate the surplus liquid.

STRAINING

Q *Does it matter if I use a nylon or wire sieve when straining fruit?*

A It is better to use a nylon mesh sieve rather than a wire one which might taint or discolour the fruit.

SUGAR

Q *Help! I've run out of caster sugar. Can I use granulated instead?*

A Yes. Put the granulated sugar in a blender or food processor and process until more finely ground. Grind still further for icing sugar.

Q *Recipes sometimes call for vanilla sugar; how do I make it?*

A Store a whole vanilla pod in a tightly closed airtight jar or tin of caster sugar. It takes several weeks for the flavour to reach full strength but can then be used when needed.

Q *How do the various types of brown sugar vary; are they suitable for cooking?*

A Brown sugars fall into two basic categories: refined and unrefined. Those from the first group are made in this country from cane or beet sugar which is refined to produce white sugar which in turn is coloured with sugar syrup, caramel or molasses. The unrefined sugars are made from sugar cane, rather than beet, and must be labelled with their country of origin. They include light muscovado and molasses (also known as black Barbados or demerara molasses) and demerara sugar. The unrefined demerara has a sticky texture and should have the country of origin on the pack or the words 'raw cane sugar' to distinguish it from the refined version.

Nutritionally, there is very little to choose from between the groups. The main difference is in taste and colour: some unrefined sugars have a stronger, more treacly flavour and are much darker. They are ideal for rich spicy cakes such as fruit cake or gingerbread. Any light brown sugars, which have a much milder flavour, can be used in a wider range of foods.

SYRUP AND TREACLE

Q *What is the easiest way to measure syrup or treacle?*

A Weigh the tin or jar without its lid, deduct the amount needed in the recipe then spoon out from the tin or jar.

T

TEMPERATURES

Q *How do I convert Fahrenheit temperatures to Celsius (Centigrade) and vice versa?*

A Subtract 32, multiply by 5 and divide by 9. To convert Celsius temperatures to Fahrenheit, multiply by 9, divide by 5 and then add 32.

TIME-SAVING

Q *Can you give me some handy hints for saving time in the kitchen?*

A Try some of the following.

- Collect all the ingredients that you will need before you start cooking.
- Preheat the oven before starting.
- Heat the grill (broiler) until really hot before using it.
- Keep a set of measuring spoons handy. Hang them above the work surface rather than keeping them in a drawer where they are easily lost.
- For good fast results, use the right tools for the job. A good sharp cook's knife and a large chopping board are essential. Store them in a convenient place, too. Wooden spoons, for example, are useful stored, handles down, in a jar near the cooker.
- If space allows and you own one, keep the food processor on the work surface.
- Buy rinded bacon.
- Don't bother to skin garlic cloves, they will crush straight through a garlic press. Incidentally, crushing rather than chopping garlic is quicker so do invest in a garlic crusher if you don't already have one. A sturdy metal one is better than plastic.
- Buy freshly grated Parmesan cheese from a delicatessen

and store it in a covered container in the refrigerator. Cartons of grated Parmesan are a poor substitute as far as flavour is concerned.

- Make up a larger quantity of French dressing than needed so that you always have some to hand. Store it in a bottle or screw-topped jar.
- Keep seasonings near the cooker so that they are handy for use.
- Use a potato peeler with a U-shaped handle and swivel blade rather than one with an upright handle and swivel or fixed blade. It peels vegetables in minutes and is easy and comfortable to use.
- Scissors are often useful and quicker for chopping than even the sharpest of knives. Use them for snipping bacon straight into the pan, and for cutting parsley, chives, smoked salmon and glacé fruit.
- Chilled items can often be sliced or chopped more quickly than unchilled. Meat placed in the freezer for 30 minutes can be cut into thin slices or strips much more easily. Cucumbers, tomatoes and peppers (capsicums) all slice more easily if chilled first.
- Keep a bottle of ready squeezed lemon juice in the refrigerator.
- Use a can of tomatoes instead of fresh to save the time it takes to skin and chop fresh ones.
- Make up a double quantity of rubbed-in flour and fat mixture. This stores in a plastic bag in the refrigerator for many weeks and can be made into shortcrust pastry, a rubbed-in cake or a crumble when required.

V

VEGETABLES

Q *Can you tell me if frozen vegetables may be eaten without being cooked once they have been thawed?*

A All frozen vegetables have been blanched and, if allowed to thaw, are perfect for use in salads. Any vegetable that you wish may be used, tossed in French dressing or mayonnaise. You may find some vegetables, however, such as broad beans, require a few minutes' cooking, but this is purely a matter of personal taste.

Q *Sometimes recipes state using a precise weight of a vegetable. Instead of weighing them, can you give me a guide to their weight at a glance?*

A
- 1 celery stick weighs 40 g ($1\frac{1}{2}$ oz)
- 1 small onion weighs 50 g (2 oz)
- 1 medium onion weighs 75–100 g (3–4 oz)
- 1 large onion weighs 150 g (5 oz)
- 1 medium pepper (capsicum) weighs 175 g (6 oz)
- 1 medium carrot weighs 100 g (4 oz)
- 1 large carrot weighs 175 g (6 oz)
- A small bunch of fresh mint is equivalent to 60 ml (4 tbsp) chopped fresh mint.

Asparagus

Q *What is the best way to cook asparagus?*

A Tie the asparagus into bundles and cover the tips with a cap made of kitchen foil. Wedge the bundles upright in a pan containing enough boiling water to come three quarters of the way up the stalks so that the stalks are poached and the tips steamed.

Aubergines (eggplants)

Q *How do I remove the bitterness from aubergines?*

A Slice them and sprinkle with salt. Either lay the slices out on a plate, or in layers in a bowl, sprinkling each layer with salt. Leave for 30 minutes, then rinse off with cold water and dry with absorbent kitchen paper.

Avocados

Q *Why are avocados sometimes streaked with brown when you cut them open? Have they spoiled?*

A No, they are perfectly good and the taste is not affected. The avocados have been stored at too cold a temperature.

Q *How do I speed up the ripening of an avocado?*

A Put it in a paper or plastic bag and store in a warm place.

Q *How do I stop a cut avocado from discolouring?*

A Brush the cut surfaces with lemon juice.

V

VEGETABLES

Beans

Q *How can I tell if French or runner beans are fresh when I buy them?*

A Fresh French or runner beans should break with a crisp snap.

Cabbage

Q *Is it possible to reduce the smell of boiling cabbage?*

A Add a little lemon juice to the cooking water.

Capsicums, see Peppers

Cauliflower

Q *How do I take away the smell of boiling cauliflower?*

A Adding a bay leaf to the simmering water will help.

Celeriac

Q *How do I stop celeriac from discolouring when I've prepared it?*

A As you prepare celeriac, drop it straight into a bowl of water to which you have added a little lemon juice.

Chicory (endive)

Q *Is it possible to tell if chicory will be bitter when buying it?*

A Chicory with green tips will be very bitter.

Chillies

Q *How should I prepare chillies?*

A When chopping or slicing hot chillies, remember to use either rubber gloves or to cover your hands in fine plastic bags. If you do touch the chillies, avoid rubbing your eyes until after you have washed your hands.

Eggplants, see Aubergines

Endive, see Chicory

Garlic

Q *How can I give just a subtle garlic flavour to a salad?*

A Rub the inside of the salad bowl with a cut clove before putting in the salad.

Q *When I fry garlic it sometimes tastes bitter; why is this?*

A Garlic turns bitter if you fry it for too long. The same applies to spices.

Q *How do you crush garlic when you haven't got a garlic press?*

A Lay an unskinned clove on a board and crush with one sharp blow with the flat of a knife. Remove the skin, which slides off easily, and finely chop the garlic. Sprinkle with salt to draw out the juices and crush with the knife.

Leeks

Q *What is the best way to get leeks really clean?*

A Wash them *after* slicing. If they are to be cooked whole, slice the leeks in half lengthways, leaving them hinged on one side, and to within 2.5 cm (1 inch) of the base. Fan out the layers of leek under running cold water to clean thoroughly.

Lettuce

Q *How do I prevent the lettuce in a salad from going brown?*

A If the lettuce has been chilled, it will brown and wilt quickly after cutting. Instead, *break* it into pieces.

Mushrooms

Q *What is the best way to prepare mushrooms?*

A It is best to wipe them, not wash them, as they absorb a lot of water. Don't peel them unless absolutely necessary as much of their goodness is in the skin.

Q *What is the best way to store mushrooms?*

A Store them in a paper, not plastic, bag in the salad drawer of the refrigerator.

Olives

Q *How should I store olives?*

A A slice of lemon placed over the surface of the olives in the jar will help to keep them fresh. They should be kept in a cool place, preferably the refrigerator.

Onions

Q *I find it difficult to skin pickling onions. Is there an easy method?*

A Plunge them quickly into hot water (just off the boil), then into cold, before skinning.

Q *How can I brown onions more quickly?*

A Add a little sugar to the frying pan.

Q *How can I avoid crying when I chop onions?*

A Skinning onions under cold water helps prevent your eyes from smarting, and so does leaving the root end on, to hold the layers together, until you've sliced both ways.

Q *When I add onions to a stuffing, must I cook them first?*

A Yes. Before adding onions to a stuffing, always part-cook them as the stuffing will never reach a high enough temperature to cook them thoroughly.

Q *How can I remove the smell of onions from my wooden chopping board?*

A Rub over it with the cut surface of a lemon.

Peas

Q *How much weight is lost from peas when they are podded?*

A 450 g (1 lb) fresh peas will yield 225 g (8 oz) when podded.

Q *How can I perk up frozen peas?*

A Cook them the French way. Put them in a saucepan with a large knob of butter, some finely chopped spring onions, a firm-hearted lettuce cut into quarters, a little chicken stock, a pinch of sugar, salt and pepper, and cook for 5–10 minutes.

Peppers (capsicums)

Q *What is the best way to skin peppers?*

A To skin peppers, char them under a hot grill (broiler), turning constantly, until the skin blackens and blisters. Plunge them straight into cold water, then rub off the skins.

Potatoes

Q *Please can you give me some hints for making good roast potatoes?*

A
- Do not over-cook the potatoes when you parboil them. The idea is not to begin cooking them but just to heat them through to speed up roasting. Over-boiled potatoes become soft at the edges and do not roast well.
- Drain the boiled potatoes well, then return them to the hot pan over a low heat to dry for a few minutes.
- For really crisp roast potatoes, rough the surfaces with a fork after boiling.
- Add the potatoes to hot dripping in a separate tin from the roast.

Q *Are green potatoes dangerous—and what causes discoloration?*

A Like many foods, potatoes contain substances which are toxic if eaten in very large quantities but completely harmless when consumed in normal amounts. One of these is alpha solanine and in some conditions (drought, extremes of temperature and exposure to light) the level of this substance increases, and the potato develops the green colour. Eating green potatoes can result in stomach upsets: the simple solution is to cut away the green parts and any shoots (these have high concentrations of alpha solanine). Potatoes that are green throughout should be discarded. To prevent the build up of solanine levels, store potatoes in a cool, dry, dark place.

Q *How do I stop fried potatoes from spattering?*

A Dry them thoroughly before frying.

Q *How long do new potatoes keep?*

A New potatoes don't store well. Never buy more than 3 days' supply at a time.

Q *What is the easiest way to scrape new potatoes?*

A New potatoes are easier to scrape if you soak them first in warm water for a few minutes.

Q *Can I speed up the cooking time of jacket potatoes?*

A Yes. If you don't own a microwave, pricking potatoes with a fork helps them bake more quickly, and also prevents them bursting. Cooking them with a skewer inserted through them also speeds up the cooking time.

Q *How do I make jacket potatoes crisp?*

A Brush them with oil, then rub the skins with salt before baking.

Q *Is it best to peel or scrub potatoes?*

A Invest in a vegetable brush. More fibre is retained in vegetables such as potatoes and carrots if they are scrubbed rather than peeled. If you do peel, use a proper swivel peeler so that only a very thin layer is removed.

Spinach

Q *If I replace fresh spinach with frozen spinach in a recipe, how much should I use?*

A 225 g (8 oz) frozen spinach is equivalent to 450 g (1 lb) fresh spinach.

Sweetcorn

Q *When I cook corn on the cob the kernels are tough. How can I prevent this?*

A Cook sweetcorn cobs lightly in *unsalted* water as salt toughens the kernels.

Tomatoes

Q *How can I avoid the acidity of canned tomatoes or tomato purée (paste) in a dish?*

A Add a pinch of sugar to counteract the acidity.

Q *How do I extract the last bit of tomato purée (paste) from the tube?*

A Use a rolling pin!

Q *What is the best way to ripen green tomatoes?*

A Put them in a warm, dark place with a ripe tomato amongst them.

Q *If I replace fresh tomatoes in a recipe with canned, what size should I use?*

A One 397 g (14 oz) can is equivalent to 450 g (1 lb) fresh tomatoes. A 227 g (8 oz) can is equivalent to 350 g (12 oz) fresh tomatoes.

Q *What is the best way to skin a tomato?*

A Put the tomato on a fork and hold it over a gas flame until the skin can be peeled off. If you haven't a gas flame, cover the tomato with boiling water and leave for about 30 seconds, then plunge straight into cold water before pulling off the skin.

Watercress

Q *What is the best way to prepare watercress?*

A When preparing watercress, do not take the elastic band off the bunch until you have chopped off the coarse stems. This saves a lot of effort.

WEIGHTS AND MEASURES

Q *Instead of weighing everything, can I measure some foods in tablespoons?*

A Yes, the following are handy tablespoon measures. Each is equivalent to 25 g (1 oz):

- Flour—$2\frac{1}{2}$ tbsp
- Rice—2 tbsp
- Cornflour, custard powder—3 tbsp
- Semolina (farina)—$2\frac{1}{2}$ tbsp
- Sugar (granulated, caster and brown)—2 tbsp
- Cocoa powder—3 tbsp
- Dried fruit (sultanas and currants)—2 tbsp
- Syrup, treacle, jam—$1\frac{1}{2}$ tbsp
- Grated cheese—3 tbsp

Q *How many teaspoons are there in a tablespoon?*

A 3 teaspoons equal 1 tablespoon.

Q *What is the most accurate way to measure ingredients?*

A
- It is always advisable to purchase a set of metric and imperial measuring spoons—imperial includes $\frac{1}{4}$ tsp, $\frac{1}{2}$ tsp, 1 tsp and 1 tbsp measures; metric spoons include 2.5 ml, 5 ml, 10 ml and 15 ml measures.
- For accuracy, always measure liquids in a measuring jug at eye level. The same applies when reading a thermometer.
- To measure dry ingredients with a spoon or cup, first scoop the ingredients lightly from the storage container, then level the surface with the edge of a straight-bladed knife.

WEIGHTS AND MEASURES, AMERICAN

Q *What is one American cup measure equivalent to?*

A For liquid measures, one American cup is equal to 225 ml (8 fl oz). For solid measures, the amount one cup contains will vary according to the ingredient. For example, 1 cup flour = 150 g (5 oz); 1 cup sugar = 200 g (7 oz). The following table lists the metric and imperial equivalent to 1 cup of many of the most frequently used ingredients.

One American cup

	Metric	**Imperial**
Allbran	65 g	$2\frac{1}{2}$ oz
Apples, cooking, peeled and sliced	100 g	4 oz
Apple sauce	225 g	8 oz
Apricots, dried	175 g	6 oz
Barley, pearl, uncooked	215 g	$7\frac{1}{2}$ oz
Barley, flakes	90 g	$3\frac{1}{2}$ oz
Bananas, mashed	225 g	8 oz
Bananas, sliced	175 g	6 oz
Beans, dried—eg, black-eye, butter	175 g	6 oz
Biscuit crumbs—eg Digestive	100 g	4 oz
Breadcrumbs, dried	140 g	$4\frac{1}{2}$ oz
Breadcrumbs, fresh	50 g	2 oz
Bran, natural wheat	50 g	2 oz
Butter (2 US 'sticks')	225 g	8 oz

Cabbage, raw, shredded	100 g	4 oz
Carrot, medium, raw, sliced	150 g	5 oz
Cheese, cottage	225 g	8 oz
Cheddar, coarsely grated and tightly packed	100 g	4 oz
Cream, curd	225 g	8 oz
Parmesan, grated	100 g	4 oz
Cherries, whole, glâcé	200 g	7 oz
Chestnuts, fresh, shelled	200 g	7 oz
Chestnuts, dried	175 g	6 oz
Cocoa powder	100 g	4 oz
Coconut, desiccated	90 g	$3\frac{1}{2}$ oz
Cornflour	140 g	$4\frac{1}{2}$ oz
Cornflakes	25 g	1 oz
Cranberries	100 g	4 oz
Cream, single, double, whipping	225 ml	8 fl oz
Currants, dried	150 g	5 oz
Dates, whole, dried, stoned	175 g	6 oz
Figs, dried	175 g	6 oz
Flour, plain, self-raising, (sifted)	150 g	5 oz
Flour, wholemeal	150 g	5 oz
Honey	350 g	12 oz
Jam	350 g	12 oz
Lard, dripping	225 g	8 oz
Lentils	200 g	7 oz
Macaroni, uncooked	100 g	4 oz
Marmalade	300 g	11 oz
Mayonnaise	225 g	8 oz
Milk, fresh	225 ml	8 fl oz
Milk, evaporated	250 ml	9 fl oz
Milk, condensed	300 ml	11 fl oz
Milk, powdered, low-fat	90 g	$3\frac{1}{2}$ oz
Mincemeat	300 g	11 oz
Mixed peel, loosely packed	175 g	6 oz
Mushrooms, fresh, sliced	50 g	2 oz
Mushrooms, canned, drained	225 g	8 oz
Muesli	150 g	5 oz
Noodles, uncooked	75 g	3 oz
Nuts, almonds, whole blanched	150 g	5 oz
flaked	100 g	4 oz
nibbed	150 g	5 oz
ground	90 g	$3\frac{1}{2}$ oz
Nuts, Brazils, whole, shelled	150 g	5 oz
Nuts, cashews, whole, shelled	150 g	5 oz
Nuts, hazelnuts, whole, shelled	150 g	5 oz
Nuts, peanuts, roasted, salted	150 g	5 oz
Nuts, walnuts, halved	100 g	4 oz
Oats, rolled	75 g	3 oz

Oils	225 ml	8 fl oz
Olives, green, stuffed	150 g	5 oz
Olives, ripe, black	175 g	6 oz
Onions, chopped	150 g	5 oz
Peaches, fresh, sliced	150 g	5 oz
Peaches, canned, sliced, drained	225 g	8 oz
Peas, frozen	100 g	4 oz
Peas, split, dried	200 g	7 oz
Peppers, sliced	100 g	4 oz
Potatoes, raw, diced	175 g	6 oz
Potatoes, cooked, mashed	225 g	8 oz
Prunes, dried	200 g	7 oz
Prunes, cooked, stoned	225 g	8 oz
Raisins, seedless	165 g	5½ oz
Rhubarb, raw, sliced	200 g	7 oz
Rice, long grain, uncooked	200 g	7 oz
Rice, short grain, uncooked	215 g	7½ oz
Sago	190 g	6½ oz
Salmon, canned, drained and flaked	175 g	6 oz
Semolina	190 g	6½ oz
Spaghetti, broken, uncooked	100 g	4 oz
Strawberries, fresh whole	150 g	5 oz
Suet, shredded	100 g	4 oz
Sugars, granulated	200 g	7 oz
caster	200 g	7 oz
icing	100 g	4 oz
soft brown, solidly packed	215 g	7½ oz
demerara	200 g	7 oz
Sultanas	175 g	6 oz
Syrup, treacle	350 g	12 oz
Tapioca	175 g	6 oz
Tomatoes, canned with juice	225 g	8 oz
Tomatoes, fresh, peeled and quartered	150 g	5 oz
Tuna fish, canned, drained and flaked	200 g	7 oz

WHEAT

Q *Are bulgar wheat and cracked wheat the same thing?*

A No, don't confuse cracked wheat with bulgar wheat. Cracked wheat is, as the name infers, lightly crushed and needs a little cooking. Bulgar is ready-processed—cooked and dried, then broken into different textures. It only needs to be soaked until it swells, then drained and the surplus moisture squeezed out before serving.

Y

YEAST

Q *Can I use dried (active dry) yeast to replace fresh yeast in a recipe and, if so, how much?*

A Yes, dried yeast can replace fresh yeast. 25 g (1 oz) fresh yeast is equivalent to 15 ml (1 level tbsp) dried yeast, plus the pinch of sugar needed to activate it.

Q *How long will fresh yeast keep?*

A Fresh yeast will keep in a loosely tied plastic bag, sealed container or kitchen foil for 3–4 weeks in the refrigerator.

YOGURT

Q *On cartons of yogurt it sometimes says it is 'live'. Is this yogurt different from others?*

A All yogurt is 'live' unless it has been pasteurised after the milk has been turned into yogurt. Most commercially produced natural yogurts are 'live' and can therefore be used as a 'starter' for making home-made yogurt.

Q *Can I substitute yogurt for cream to reduce the calories/kilojoules in recipes?*

A Yes. Use yogurt to replace cream in salad dressings, chilled soups, sauces, dips, desserts and ice cream.

Q *Can I use yogurt in cooked dishes?*

A Yogurt can be used in cooking, but bring it to room temperature before using it in hot dishes. Stir it into the dish gradually and do not allow it to boil or it will curdle.

Q *My home-made yogurt is watery. What should I do to improve it?*

A Try adding 15 ml (1 level tbsp) dried skimmed milk, dissolved in a little warmmilk, at the start of making your yogurt.

YORKSHIRE PUDDING

Q *My Yorkshire pudding doesn't rise. What can I do?*

A Just add an extra egg to the recipe and you'll be amazed by the result!

Q *I'm often very disappointed with my Yorkshire pudding. Can you suggest what I might be doing wrong?*

A The following are causes of common problems.

- *Soggy, heavy or tough*: Batter too thick; tin too small; oven too cool; fat too cool.
- *Insufficiently risen*: Batter too thin; too little egg; oven too cool; pudding too low in oven.

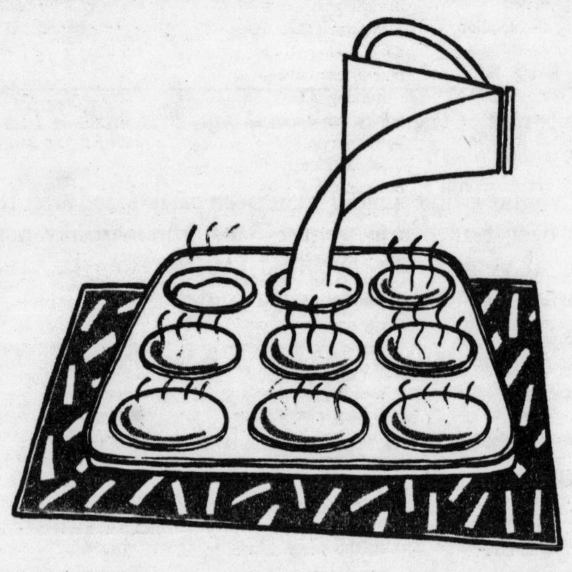

INDEX